Hg2 Los Angeles

A Hedonist's guide to
Los Angeles

Written by Andrew Stone

Photographed by Ian Burnap

A HEDONIST'S GUIDE TO LOS ANGELES

MANAGING DIRECTOR – Tremayne Carew Pole
MARKETING DIRECTOR – Sara Townsend
SERIES EDITOR – Catherine Blake
DESIGN – Katy Platt
MAPS – Amber Sheers & Nick Randall
REPRO – Advantage Digital Print
PRINTER – Leo Paper
PUBLISHER – Filmer Ltd

Additional photography – Tom Shelby (Gordon Ramsay), Lisa Thompson (Jar),
Richard Carroll (Play Intro), Noa Montes (Osteria Mozza), Glenn Cormier
(West Hollywood), Darryl Verret (Saints and Sinners), LA Inc, Beverly Hills TCB,
Santa Monica TCB, West Hollywood TCB

Email – info@hg2.com
Website – www.hg2.com

Published in the United Kingdom in January 2009 by
Filmer Ltd
17 Shawfield Street
London SW3 4BA

ISBN – 978-1-905428-25-0

Hg2 Los Angeles

CONTENTS

How to…

A Hedonist's guide to Los Angeles is broken down into easy to use sections: Sleep, Eat, Drink, Snack, Party, Culture, Shop, Play and Info. In each section you'll find detailed reviews and photographs. At the front of the book is an introduction to the city and an overview map, followed by introductions to the five main areas and more detailed maps. On each of these maps the places we have featured are laid out by section, highlighted on the map with a symbol and a number. To find out about a particular place simply turn to the relevant section, where all entries are listed alphabetically. Alternatively, browse through a specific section (e.g. Eat) until you find a restaurant you like the look of. Surrounding your choice will be a coloured box – each colour refers to a particular area of the city. Simply turn to the relevant map to find the location.

Book your hotel on Hg2.com

We believe that the key to a great city break is choosing the right hotel. Our unique site now enables you to browse through our selection of hotels, using the interactive maps to give you a good feel for the area as well as the nearby restaurants, bars, sights, etc., before you book. Hg2 has formed partnerships with the hotels featured in our guide to bring them to readers at the lowest possible price. Our site now incorporates special offers from selected hotels, as well as a diary of interesting events taking place, 'Inspire Me'.

The concept

A Hedonist's guide to Los Angeles is designed to appeal to quirky, urbane and the incredibly stylish traveller. The kind of person interested in gourmet food, elegant hotels, hip clubs and seriously chic bars – someone who feels the need to explore, shop and pamper themselves away from the crowds.

We give you an insider's knowledge of Los Angeles; we want you to feel like an in-the-know local, and to take you to the most fashionable and hippest places in town to rub shoulders with the scenesters and glitterati alike.

Work so often rules our life, and weekends away are few and far between; when we do manage to break away we want to have as much fun and to relax as much as possible with the minimum amount of stress. This guide is all about maximizing time. The photographs of every place we feature help you to make a quick choice and fit in with your own style.

Unlike many other people we pride ourselves on our independence and our integrity. We eat in all the restaurants, drink in all the bars, and go wild in the nightclubs – all totally incognito. We charge no one for the privilege of appearing in the guide, and every place is reviewed and included at our discretion.

Cities are best enjoyed by soaking up the atmosphere: wander the streets, indulge in some retail therapy, re-energize yourself with a massage and then get ready to eat and party yourself into a stupor.

Los Angeles

There are a million songs that mention Los Angeles… 'Hotel California,' 'Hollywood Nights,' 'Nobody Walks in LA,' 'Peace Frog,' 'Welcome to the Jungle.' Why? Because no place on earth is as cinematic, decadent, indulgent, freaky, fabulous, transporting, or unlikely as this sprawling metropolis, home to nearly 4 million people and the second largest city in the US. Here in the City of Angels – we like to call is Lalaland – the entertainment industry reigns supreme, and indeed you will find all those caricatures associated with it lurking around every corner: the Venice beach hippie, the plastic surgery-addicted trophy wife, the Bentley-driving studio executive, the ultra-glamorous movie star. Thankfully, there are plenty of regular people, too – though we wouldn't exactly call them 'average Joes'… Everyone drawn to this city has a big dream, be it the shop girl with an album to record, the bartender with a screenwriting degree, the short order cook with designs on becoming the next big restaurateur, the med student who can't wait to start offering starlets new noses… this list goes on forever, as well it should. Dreams become reality in Los Angeles when you least expect it… and if they don't at least the weather is marvelous.

Yes, the weather… With 325 sunny days a year, LA is considered to have a Mediterranean climate, and is located in the 'Dry-Summer' subtropical zone. What this means is: rent a convertible, people. It's mild and cosseting during the day and cool and cozy at night, so no wonder Angelenos have mastered the art of dressing casually. Health reigns supreme in this town, and the beauty standard is extraordinarily high, so fitness is a big part of most people's daily routine – be it at the gym, yoga, hiking in Runyon Canyon (entrances are at Vista and Fuller in Hollywood), beach volleyball, tennis, or swimming (yes, the fabled LA pool boys do exist). You will probably notice the results the second you step off the plane… long-legged beauties and chiseled heartthrobs are the city's unofficial mascots.

Your eyes will have a feast as you cruise around LA… Along the boule-
vards you'll see a million fast food restaurants (an irony, given the general obsession with 'skinny'), many prominent religious buildings (from
Roman Catholic, Buddhist, Islamic, and Eastern Orthodox to more
newsworthy practices such at Kabbalah and the Church of Scientology),
great stretches of shopping, restaurants with their valet parking stands

out front, tons of wacky storefronts, and, of course, the iconic palm
trees that symbolize the city's lush, sun-soaked lifestyle. It's a hoot to
cruise through the residential neighborhoods of Beverly Hills; it's every
bit as glamorous as you're imagining… Though LA is also a great town
to raise kids – and there are many – so drive slowly. While Rodeo Drive
is of course home to the most luxurious shops in the world, you'll also
love the Sunset Strip, Melrose, Robertson, Larchmont, Beverly, La Brea,
Westwood Village, Santee Alley in Downtown LA, the 3rd Street
Promenade in Santa Monica.

Beyond that, you're bound to have a great time if you can calm your
nerves as the locals do, let the pace and vibe of the city direct you, and
take advantage of the myriad magical surprises that cross your path. The
hotels are world-class, the food scene is outrageously good, the nightlife
rivals that of any major city in the world (thanks to the sybaritic and
gorgeous population), the sites are begging to be enjoyed, and so much
more.

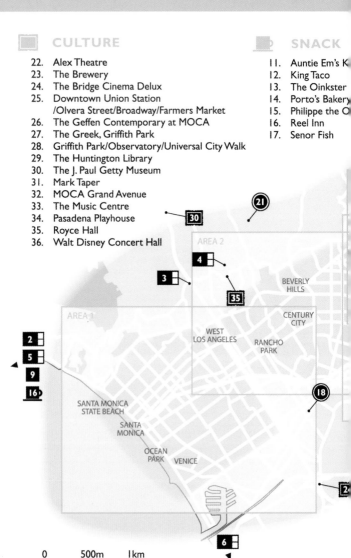

SLEEP

1. Millenium Biltmore Hotel
2. Casa Malibu Inn
3. Hotel Angeleno
4. Hotel Bel-Air
5. Malibu Beach Inn
6. The Shade Hotel

EAT

7. Sushi Nozawa

PARTY

18. Backstage Bar & Grill
19. The Edison
20. Sam's Hofbrau
21. Vibrato Grill Jazz ... Etc

DRINK

8. Firefly
9. Moonshadows Blue Lounge
10. NoBar

West Hollywood, Hollywood, and Studio City

If you really want to be in the middle of the action, throw yourself smack bang in the center of the city, where the stars come out to play, true movie history resides, the Scientologists try to convert you, and the freaks come out at night. To the rest of the world, 'Hollywood' means the movie business, and Tinseltown doesn't like to disappoint. It's home to the Hollywood Walk of Fame, Amoeba Music (the greatest record store of all time), the Arclight theater complex, Grauman's Chinese Theater, and the Kodak Theater, where the Oscars are held. Paramount is the only fully functioning major movie studio still in Hollywood, and its fenced-in lot and iconic water tower are a thrill to behold for any true film fanatic. Most importantly, there is a drive-through In-n-Out Burger on Sunset and Orange, and we can't go too long without one of those incredible little suckers.

At night, Hollywood becomes party central, and people come from far and wide to get their drink on. There are so many sights to behold – meaning spectacular décor and cha-cha patrons. Some of our favorite spots these days: Beauty Bar, Spider Club, Knitting Factory, and The Avalon. There are a million great ways to show off your stuff, get an eyeful of naughty behavior, and imbibe like it was going out of style.

Moving away from the raw nerve that is Hollywood, we have West Hollywood. WeHo is super diverse and vibrant, with iconic thoroughfares, peaceful residential neighborhoods, nightclubs, bars, cool restaurants, the Pacific Design Center (a.k.a. the Big Blue Whale), great shopping, the most high profile stretch of hotels ever, performance venues, many Russians, and a buzzing gay scene. If you want to see something hilarious, spend a bit of time at The Target on La Brea and Santa Monica… For some reason it is eye candy central, and you never know what kind of hoity-toit can be found picking through the Method soap and designer duds-for-less.

As mentioned, this is known as 'Boy's Town,' and for good reason. While there are gay people all over town (and they arguably run a lot of the movie business), this is what we call the 'gay ghetto.' Our all time favorite gay bar is called Fubar, on Santa Monica and Crescent Heights. The owner, Jay, is a painfully handsome (straight) boxer who delivers a super-hunky staff and a delightfully down-and-dirty good time environment. For a straighter, but not narrower evening of sex appeal, hit the revamped Viper Room (8852 Sunset Boulevard) for loud music and a foxy crowd.

When you aren't chasing tail, the Sunset Strip's a fab place to pray to the fashion gods. Many top brands have outposts here, though we suggest above all that you stop in at uber-boutique Tracey Ross. Tracey herself often holds court, and she and her staff deliver style advice you won't find anywhere else. Celeb-centric hotels like the mythic Chateau Marmont, the sleek Mondrian, the impeccable Sunset Tower (formerly the Argyle), and the rocker-fave Sunset Marquis all can be found here, too.

Basically, if you aren't stimulated in these 'hoods, it's your problem, not theirs.

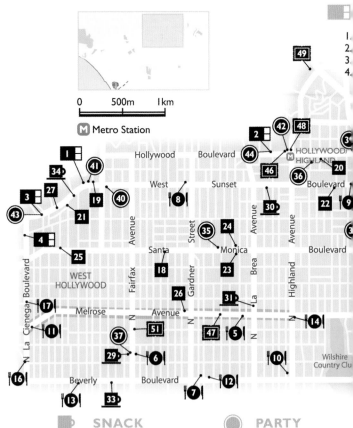

0   500m   1km

M Metro Station

Hollywood   Boulevard

West   Sunset

Santa   Monica

Melrose   Avenue

Beverly   Boulevard

Avenue   Street   Avenue   Avenue

Fairfax   Gardner   Brea   La   Highland

La Cienega   Boulevard

WEST
HOLLYWOOD

Boulevard

HOLLYWOOD/
HIGHLAND

Boulevard

Wilshire
Country Clu

LEEP

- hateau Marmont
- ollywood Roosevelt Hotel
- he Mondrian
- unset Marquis Hotel

EAT

5. Alll'Angelo
6. Animal
7. BLD
8. Cheebo
9. Citrus at Social
10. Cobras & Matadors
11. Comme Ça
12. Grace
13. Jar
14. Osteria Mozza
15. Providence
16. Sona
17. STK

DRINK

18. Bar Lubitsch
19. Bar Marmont
20. Boardner's
21. Cabo Cantina on Sunset
22. Cat & Fiddle
23. Formosa Café
24. Jones
25. Marix Tex-Mex Café
26. Snake Pit
27. Tower Bar at Sunset Tower Hotel
28. The Well

50

Hollywood

M HOLLYWOOD/ VINE

5

32

28

N Gower Street

Street

Place

Freeway

Vine

Wilton

N Western Avenue

Avenue

Melrose

N

BEVERLY/ VERMONT
M

Beverly   Boulevard

CULTURE

45. Arclight
46. El Capitan
47. The Groundling's Theater
48. Hollywood and Highland Chinese Theater
49. Hollywood Bowl
50. Pantages
51. Silent Movie Theatre

SHOP

Melrose Ave

elt

Beverly Hills, Bel Air, and Westwood

Nowhere on earth are the locals ritzier, the establishments glitzier, the mansions more monstrous, the cars more souped-up, or the shopping and dining more decadent than in Beverly Hills. Famous from *90210*, *Beverly Hills Cop*, *The Beverly Hillbillies*, and such, this place is simply synonymous with 'rich.' Rodeo Drive's boutiques are the most dazzling. The hotels are legendary. The residents are really loaded, and often artificially augmented. All this said, there is plenty for mere mortals to do, so don't be intimidated.

Get the lay of the land by cruising up and down some of the residential streets... Burton Way is the best of the bunch, with its dramatic lines of palm trees and outrageous homes. You'll notice that there's no shortage of work for gardeners and landscape architects. There are constantly crews working on the shrubs and grass, plus pool boys skimming the water out back. (Yes, what you suspect about bored housewives and fit, young pool boys is probably truer than you think. There's a whole lot of naughty going on all over this city... People are beautiful, and not wearing much, and bored. You do the math.)

OK. Now, shop talk. David Yurman, Christian Dior, Montblanc, Yves Saint Laurent, Valentino, Van Cleef & Arpels... It's luxury brand-a-go-go and we likey. Even if you can't afford more than some shoelaces from Niketown, it's an experience you don't want to miss. Here's a tip... Dress up, up, up when you hit these stores, and don't forget the highest end accessories you've got in your arsenal. The shop girls and boutique boys are highly trained to notice your belts, shoes, bags, and jewelry, which will then determine the level of service you receive. (It's not fair, but it's the way of the world...)

Next up is Bel Air. It's not really a gated community, but the faux gate at Sunset and Bellagio gets the point across: really, really mega-rich people live here. Multi-family housing isn't permitted, and there are

strict rules about building and landscaping that shan't be broken for anyone. The third point in the so-called 'Platinum Triangle' is Holmby Hills. (Beverly Hills, Bel Air, Holmby Hills. La, di, da.) This is one of our most favorite spots, because Hugh Hefner lives here, in the Playboy Mansion. Being invited to a party at the Playboy Mansion is the greatest honor known to man, and if you happen to be invited to one while you are in town, go. Mind your P's and Q's, however… Rabble-rousers are unceremoniously tossed out on their behinds.

So, you get the point. It's 'that' version of the American dream… the one where you've got a Rolls-Royce, and a butler, and a house like Daddy Warbucks, and a choice of swimming pools, and so on and so forth. It has come alive in full color, and you are free to drive through it. Own the experience, we say… Don't shrink at the sight of Victoria Beckham. Don't ask her to sign your cleavage, either, But hopefully that goes without saying.

PARTY

SHOP

CULTURE

Beverly Hills, Bel Air, Westwood local map

SLEEP

1. Avalon Hotel
2. Beverly Hills Hotel & Bungalow
3. Beverly Wilyshire Hotel
4. Four Seasons Hotel
5. London West Hollywood
6. Maison 140
7. The Mosaic Hotel
8. The Peninsula Beverly Hills
9. Raffles L'Ertmitage
10. W Hotel Westwood

EAT

11. Belvedere at the Peninsula
12. Crustacean
13. Cut at Beverly Wiltshire Hotel
14. Dominick's
15. Gordon Ramsay at the London West Hollywood
16. The Ivy
17. Nobu Los Angeles
18. Spago

DRINK

19. The Abbey
20. Bar Noir at Maison 140
21. Dan Tana's
22. Maestro's
23. The Polo Lounge

SNACK

24. Apple Pan
25. Urth Café

Santa Monica, Venice, and Brentwood

There's much beachy goodness to be found on the city's sparkling, famous west side. Hell, you may just want to book into Shutters on the Beach and skip all the sightseeing in the rest of the city altogether. Not that we recommend that, necessarily, but it's just groovy and exhilarating by the water, and we wouldn't blame you. So much has happened here; so many have been inspired by the culture and lifestyle. It's where the beat poets flourished back in the day. Hippies still roam free. The Red Hot Chili Peppers started off as munchkin troublemakers on this sand. It's a way of living that just doesn't seem reasonable anywhere else… but somehow these wacky, wonderful communities manage to make it work.

Downtown Venice is a total pleasure, with plenty of unlikely little shops, cafés, and bars dotting Abbot Kinney Boulevard and the surrounding area. Along Venice Beach, you'll get an eyeful, for sure. One truly outrageous destination: Muscle Beach. Bodybuilders have long flocked here to get huge under the hot sun. Now-Governor Arnold Schwarzenegger could often be found out there 'pomping ahp,' and some of the photos from the 1980s are pretty awesome to gaze upon. In addition, you can see the streetballers take each other on in intense outdoor basketball games, a scene immortalized in the better-than-it-should-have-been movie *White Men Can't Jump*. Other fun spectacles are: the skate dancers, handball, and many tan, beautiful people playing beach volleyball. It's all very Matthew McConnaughey. (Good to know, in case you run into a malady of some sort while you are here: The Venice Family Clinic at 604 Rose Avenue is the largest free clinic in the country. It happens to the best of us.) OK, enough about Venice.

Santa Monica has long been the nucleus of the skating and surfing worlds, and was famously dubbed 'Dogtown' back in the day. (You may have seen the movie *Lords of Dogtown*… probably not.) Now, however, big money reigns supreme in this area, and that old, gritty, anything-

could-happen vibe has been replaced by an "I'll have an iced soy Chai" mentality. Ah well. The Santa Monica Pier is a perfect way to while away an evening, with the huge Ferris wheel, a 1920s carousel, an aquarium, a hopping arcade, and some family friendly spots for junk food. And the Third Street Promenade is choc-a-bloc with standard favorite shops and cafés (Urban Outfitters, Starbucks, Armani Exchange, Barnes & Noble, etc.).

The Pacific Palisades is nestled atop Santa Monica, and Palisades Park offers exquisite views from its bluffs. Brentwood is quite a different story altogether… Ritzy yet removed from the Hollywood madness, it is home to the Governator, Steven Spielberg, Justin Timberlake, and Cindy Crawford. (Can you imagine what the grocery store lines are like?) Famously, the Santa Ana winds kicked up quite a fury in 1961 and the infamous Brentwood – Bel Air fire went wild through the area and took out numbers of homes, including those of Burt Lancaster and Zsa Zsa Gabor. Just thought you should know.

It's bordered by the San Diego Freeway, too, so if you're feeling impulsive, just hop on, head south, and kiss Mexico for us.

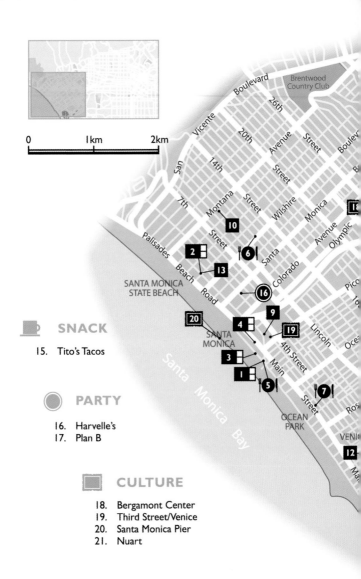

SNACK

15. Tito's Tacos

PARTY

16. Harvelle's
17. Plan B

CULTURE

18. Bergamont Center
19. Third Street/Venice
20. Santa Monica Pier
21. Nuart

Brentwood, Santa Monica, Venice local map

SLEEP

1. Casa Del Mar
2. The Huntley Hotel
3. Shutters on the Beach
4. Viceroy Santa Monica

EAT

5. Catch at Casa Del Mar
6. Mélisse
7. Via Veneto

DRINK

8. Air Conditioned
9. Cameo Bar at the Viceroy
10. Father's Office
11. Liquid Kitty
12. The Otheroom
13. Penthouse at the Huntley Hotel
14. Saints & Sinners

Hancock Park, Mid-Wilshire, and Mid-City

Wilshire is a mighty important boulevard here in LA, ya know. It goes from Grand Avenue in Downtown, all the way to Santa Monica. This area we're discussing here – west of Downtown LA, south of Hollywood, east of Beverly Hills, and north of the I-10 – is a nucleus, where different sensibilities meld, needs collide, cultures commingle, styles converge, and life happens on a grand scale.

Wilshire Boulevard, itself, has many personalities. One of its most famous stretches, between Fairfax and La Brea, is called the Miracle Mile. Here, you'll find both LACMA (the Los Angeles County Museum of Art) and the La Brea Tar Pits museum, as well as numerous commercial high rises (the only ones of its kind in town). It's a neat part of town, teeming with life and culture. Total overgeneralization: the people around here aren't as ostentatious as they are in other parts of town.

Larchmont, or Larchmont Village, is absolutely charming, and a definite must-do during your visit. Technically in Windsor Square and close to Hancock Park, it's a sweet main street that conjures small town USA in a way, with coffee shops, clothes shops, bookstores, juice and bagel joints. What isn't so 'small town' is the fact that you may be ordering a latte next to one of the cast members of *Friends*... Be cautious while cruising that you don't drive through a crosswalk while someone is walking... They have utter right of way here and you'll get a fine plus nasty looks. There is metered parking along the way, plus garage parking, though if you drive a little past the business area, you can find some free street parking.

Oh, while we're on the subject of Larchmont: LA isn't known for its pizza, but the Village Pizzeria is super authentic, and their ham and pineapple slices are a little trip to heaven. Le Petit Greek is always busy in the al fresco section, and the ouzo-flamed cheese is as dramatic as it is addictively delicious… Waiters set your cheese ablaze, caus-

ing heads to turn and get jealous of you with your fire-blessed goodness. Across the street, the scene at the Larchmont's Peet's coffee makes for really great people-watching, so park yourself at one of the benches out front and observe (but don't ogle). Maybe you can finally put pen to paper and get going on that screenplay about some person who vaguely resembles you doing similar things to those you've done in your own life.

Moving on… Koreatown is dense and big. Outside of Asia, Greater LA is home to the largest number of ethnic Koreans, and this is the densest concentration of Korean businesses. Be warned, the signs are mostly in Korean, so unless that's your second language, you'll have to guess. The community is extremely tight knit and the culture well preserved, which adds a vital, vibrant element to town. In contrast, Hancock Park is like the suburbs plopped down in the middle of the city, and it's pretty darn pleasant to visit. The homes are set far back from the street, with actual lawns in front! Wow.

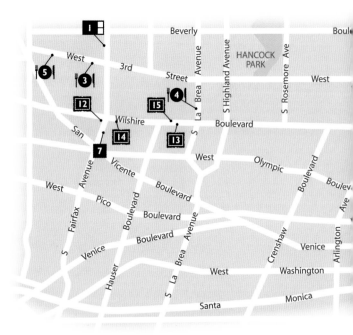

DRINK

6. Golden Gopher
7. Tom Bergin's Tavern

0   1km   2km

Ⓜ Metro Station

BEVERLY/
VERMONT
Ⓜ

West
Hollywood
Temple
Street
Freeway

Beverly
Boulevard

West 3rd St

Street
WILTSHIRE/
'SHIRE/ NORMANDIE
STERN Ⓜ Wilshire

Avenue

S Virgil Avenue

S Rampart Blvd

Avenue

Lucas Ave

Freeway

WEST LAKE
MC ARTHUR PARK
Ⓜ

West
Boulevard

West 6th Street

10

Vermont

Hoover Street

8th
Street

Irolo Street

Western

South

South

Pico
Boulevard
Boulevard

Boulevard

oulevard

Freeway

S Union Avenue

Pasadena

16

8

6

2

11

Ⓜ 7TH STREET
METRO CENTER

CULTURE

12. Acme
13. Ace Institute of Contemporary Art
14. Los Angeles County Museum of Art (LACMA)
15. El Ray
16. Staples Centre

Los Feliz, Silverlake, Echo Park, and East

If Beverly Hills is a bejeweled heiress, and Venice a well-moisturized yoga bunny, then the east side of LA could be seen as a tattooed power babe who makes waves all day and knows how to live it up in style at night. Once you drive through Hollywood and all that frenetic loveliness, you'll find yourself in cooler, edgier territory... a weird and wooly world full of delights, surprises, oddities; an amazing fusion of scruffy haired insouciance and straight-up, orange-pickin', Californian sun worship.

Yes, on the far side of the 101, hip and hyper-creative folks have set up camp in what many consider to be the 'East Village of LA.' Artists, rockers, and young celebs cluster at any number of relaxed hot spots. (We particularly love Alcove on Hillhurst, where the lines don't lie, and Fred 62 on Vermont, where we get to flirt with punk rock waitresses while devouring a 'Fred MacMurray' egg sandwich at an ungodly hour.) Quality carousing can happen on any corner, and it's always fun just to cruise around, checking out the charming houses built into the craggy sloping streets.

Design nuts will be excited to spy Richard Neutra's Lovell House or Frank Lloyd Wright's Ennis House and Hollyhock House. FYI, LA is a Mecca for aspiring architects, and there are important structures here, there, and everywhere. Once you get into the Hollywood Hills, which overlook Griffith Park, there are celebrities around every corner, literally, and have been since pictures started moving. Most exciting for some, you'll find Griffith Park, with over 4,210 acres of landmarked parkland – an expansive stretch of 'urban wilderness' (the largest in the US) and playing/picnicking spots galore. Here you can peep the

Hollywood sign like nowhere else before checking out the historic Griffith Observatory, one of the city's most iconic spots and a world-recognized leader in astrological research. Beyond that, there's swimming, tennis, horseback riding, golf, hiking, the LA Zoo, and the charming Griffith Merry-Go-Round. Maximum relaxation before a sinful night out.

And there's plenty of sin to be found... but it's not all déclassé the way it can be in other parts of town. Spaceland hosts incredible live music, and has been the launching pad for many a now-famous band. The Drawing Room is a prime spot for a sexy, low-lit interlude. Further out in Eagle Rock, we like CT Lounge on Colorado. For the same-sex oriented, you've got Akbar (the ultimate indie gay bar), the Faultline (a rough leather joint that hosts the most entertaining Sunday al fresco beer blast ever), and MJ's (for go-go boys and killer crowds).

So, if you're bored with all that Walk of Fame stuff, don't feel like maxing out another credit card on Rodeo Drive, and can't make any more strolls up and down the 3rd Street Promenade, shake up your experience with a trip over this way. It's an area many visitors overlook, but brims with so many possibilities. Yes, the locals look intimidating and cutting edge, but they tend to be pretty chill. Just be yourself and you'll get along fine.

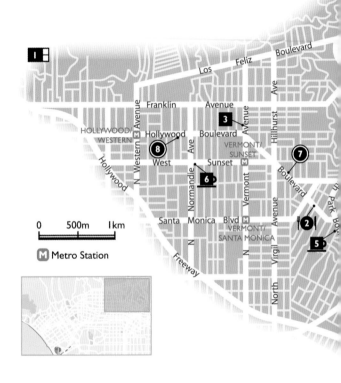

0   500m   1km

Ⓜ Metro Station

Los Feliz, Silverlake, Koreatown, Echo Park, and east local map

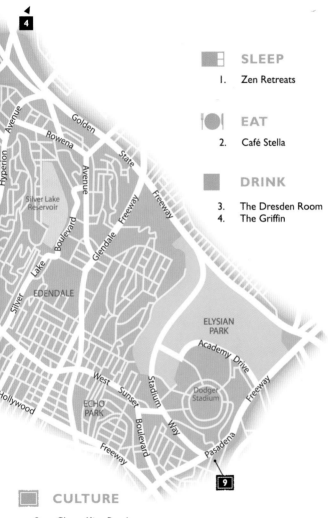

SLEEP
1. Zen Retreats

EAT
2. Café Stella

DRINK
3. The Dresden Room
4. The Griffin

CULTURE
9. Chung King Road

sleep...

Hotels in Los Angeles rarely enjoy the kind of worshipful veneration reserved for lodgings in other cities around the world. But when you really think about it, without its hotels, which have been central to its mythmaking, LA might be a very different place indeed.

Take, for example, the now-extinct Hollywood Hotel, built in 1902 as a luxe lure to sell neighboring residential lots among the lemon groves in the area known as Hollywood. When LA's first movie studio opened nearby in 1911, suddenly the hotel, the closest primary pampering place, became home to the influx of East Coast silent films stars and studio heads migrating west to the idyllic climate, and as they put down roots suddenly the public became very aware of this mystical region, cementing the image of Hollywood as the capital of entertainment in the public consciousness. The golden stars affixed to the hotel ceiling bearing famous names even became the basis of Hollywood Boulevard's Walk of Fame.

Similarly, the creation of the Beverly Hills Hotel in 1912 led to a land rush in the lush, pristine environs a few years later as movie stars and moguls built mammoth million-dollar mansions, looking to escape a Hollywood that had (surprise) quickly become synonymous with sex, sin, and scandal. Thus was born the legend of Beverly Hills as the rarefied residence of the biggest names in the business.

These hotels and those that followed defined the very notion of LA glamour: The Hollywood Roosevelt hosted the very first Academy Awards, succeeded by the Biltmore and the Ambassador, grafting the ultimate self-congratulatory red carpet scenario to the world's vision of LA. The tradition is upheld today by the Golden Globes, which annually invades of the Beverly Hilton, and the Oscars, now held among the Kodak Theater and Renaissance Hotel, conjoined at the epic Hollywood & Highland complex – which, incidentally, occupies the original site of the Hollywood Hotel.

With its star-filled Cocoanut Grove nightclub, the late, much lamented Ambassador contributed to the notion of a luxury LA lodging as a place where the glitterati and posing hopefuls drink, dance, and canoodle amid elegant environs. The party palace image would be reinterpreted for various eras at places like Chateau Marmont and the Hyatt House, all the way to today's Mondrian and the clubs at the Hollywood Roosevelt.

So many more essential elements of LA's iconography sprang forth from hotels. Fantasy: the Beverly Wilshire's role in the rags-to-Rodeo Drive dream of Pretty Woman. Scandal: John Belushi's drug-induced death at the Chateau Marmont. Noir: the album image of the Beverly Hills Hotel on 'Hotel California,' the Eagles' musical meditation on LA, hedonism, and soul-emptiness. Sex: Marilyn Monroe slept here, and here, and here... Urban Legend: did the Munchkin actors engage in wild booze-and-sex parties at the Culver Hotel while filming *The Wizard of Oz*? Even American Tragedy: the assassination of Robert F. Kennedy at the Ambassador.

Hollywood loves a good story, and it seems so many of them generate from its landmark hotels.

What you'll find here is a collection of some of the most enticing settings to start Act One of your LA story. Often dramatically different scenes, they all have class, style, and character in common. It's by no means a definitive list, with so many more accommodations suited to the particular tastes of the discriminating hedonist.

Some others that didn't quite fit in our list that might also suit your script: the Beverly Hilton, the Thompson, the Sofitel, the Century Plaza, the Standard on Sunset, the London, Sunset Tower, the Chamberlain, the Elan, the Georgian, the Bonaventure, the Ritz-Carlton Marina del Rey, and the bed-and-breakfasts of Pasadena. There are also some highly anticipated hotels on the immediate horizon, including the Montage and SBE Group's SLS in Beverly Hills, and the W in Hollywood.

Wherever you're checking in, you can check out any time you like but you can never leave – you'll be taking a bit of LA back with you. So welcome to the Hotel California...

Our top ten hotels in Los Angeles are:

1. Hotel Bel-Air
2. Raffles L'Ermitage
3. The Beverly Hills Hotel & Bungalows
4. The Peninsula Beverly Hills
5. Chateau Marmont
6. Four Seasons Hotel
7. Shutters on the Beach
8. The Beverly Wilshire
9. Sunset Marquis Hotel & Villas
10. Casa del Mar

Our top five hotels for style are:

1. The Shade Hotel
2. The Huntley Hotel
3. Maison 140
4. The Mosaic
5. The Viceroy

Our top five hotels for atmosphere are:

1. Chateau Marmont
2. Hotel Bel-Air
3. Hollywood Roosevelt Hotel
4. The Beverly Hills Hotel & Bungalows
5. The Huntley Hotel

Our top five hotels for location are:

1. Shutters On the Beach
2. The Beverly Hills Hotel & Bungalows
3. Beverly Wilshire
4. Casa del Mar
5. Malibu Beach Inn

The Avalon Hotel, 9400 W Olympic Blvd (Canon), Beverly Hills

Tel: 800 439 3719   www.avalonbeverlyhills.com
Rates: $289–415

Retro doesn't come any more cozy and chic than at this six-decade old hotel (Marilyn Monroe lived here in her starlet days) nestled off the Bev Hills beaten path. Designer Kelly Wearstler gave the mid-century property a modernist makeover with Asian accents alongside Eames chairs, George Nelson bubble lamps, Noguchi glass-topped tables, and a gorgeous copper-encased elevator. The rooms are appropriately posh, and the stunning centerpiece is the idyllic figure eight pool that's oh-so Melrose Place, and the adjoining 'Blue on Blue' lounge, which is ideal for cabana-side cocktailing.

Style 7, Atmosphere 7, Location 7

Beverly Hills Hotel & Bungalows, 9641 Sunset Blvd (Coldwater Canyon), Beverly Hills

Tel: 310 276 2251   www.thebeverlyhillshotel.com
Rates: $565–7,750

The standard-bearer for quintessential Hollywood glamour and luxury since 1912 – the hotel was built to lure moneyed vacationers to the region and *90210* as we know it sprung to life around it – lodgings simply do not come more iconic and old school-elegant as the five-star, Mission-style 'Pink Palace.' From its signature striped *port cochere* to its film-famous pool and tennis courts to the lavish Polo Lounge to the rapturously retro Fountain

Coffee Shop to the remarkable bungalows where the rich and famous have stayed, played, and partied with every conceivable convenience, you'll feel transported into a bygone era of power, privilege, and pampering. We could regale you endlessly with tales of the legends made there, but we suggest you create your own.

Style 8, Atmosphere 9, Location 8

Beverly Wilshire Hotel, 9500 Wilshire Blvd (Rodeo), Beverly Hills
Tel: 310 275 5200   www.fourseasons.com/beverlywilshire
Rates: $545–10,000

Beloved as the setting for *Pretty Woman*, the Beverly Wilshire remains a glorious *grand dame* after three-quarters of a century catering to globe-hoppers congregating within its Europe-meets-East-Coast flair. History abounds

(Warren Beatty bedded the world here in his bachelor heyday, as did Elvis Presley, Steve McQueen alongside an array of presidents, princes, and potentates) and amenities reign – there are the erudite charms of the original Wilshire wing, while the Beverly wing offers slightly more modern perks and proximity to the sumptuous pool and spa. The posh hotel has shucked some of its stuffiness with Wolfgang Puck's celebrated steakhouse Cut (Tom Cruise is a regular) and the busy, recently revamped streetside lounge The Blvd. Housing Escada and Mikimoto, it also enjoys across-the-street proximity to ritzy Rodeo Drive, where you can re-enact Julia Roberts' shopping spree in high style.

Style 7, Atmosphere 8, Location 9

The Millennium Biltmore Hotel, 506 S Grand Ave (5th St), Downtown

Tel: 213 624 1011 www.millenniumhotels.com
Rates: $149–5,000

No hotel better encapsulates Downtown's everything-old-is-new-again scene than the 80-year-old Biltmore, which remains a timeless bastion of elegance. Opulent in the extreme (and decidedly anti-SoCal) with its exotic

European trappings – soak in Spanish-colonial architectural details of the marble halls, sculpted columns, Pompeii-inspired Grand Ballroom, and Sistine-style painted ceilings – it's like walking through a storybook (the rooms also reflect time, though: they're early-century-smallish and not as sparkling as some more luxe digs). The atmosphere combines Hollywood history – it frequently hosted early Academy Awards ceremonies – with a tantalizing hint of noir – the legendary Black Dahlia was last seen alive in the lobby.

Style 7, Atmosphere 7, Location 6

Casa del Mar, 1910 Ocean Way (Pico), Santa Monica
Tel: 310 581 5533 www.hotelcasadelmar.com
Rates: $520–3,200

Santa Monica's centerpiece of sumptuous seaside swank since its 1920s origins as a members-only beach resort, the brick-and-sandstone structure is steps away from the Pacific shore. The expansive, multi-tiered lobby is awash in romantic high regency detailing, past the front desk, through the library, and into the deco-décor-ed Veranda Bar (a glam gathering place for guests and glittery locals alike) leading out onto a patio perfectly suited for watching the sunset over Champagne. The indulgent aquatic experience extends beyond the beach: every room comes with an Italian marble bath, and the hydrothermic spa tubs – offering views overlook the pool, and views of you if you're a bit exhibitionist – are always inhabited by a darling rubber ducky.

Style 8, Atmosphere 8, Location 9

Casa Malibu Inn, 22752 Pacific Coast Highway, Malibu
Tel: 310 456 2219
Rates: $159–499

Don't let the modest motel-like façade fool you: the vine-covered, villa-esque retreat remains a favored hideaway for out-of-towners and locals alike thanks to its away-from-it-all-but-still-having-it-all atmosphere. The cottage-like lodgings are coastline-chic with a palm tree-studded brick courtyard leading down wooden stairs to a private beach (raked smooth at sunrise) in the heart of the 'Bu's ritziest community. Half the rooms offer views of the Pacific that moguls and movie stars pay millions to obtain — even the 'garden view' rooms allow ample access to the ocean. Amenities vary from room to room, including fireplaces, private decks, kitchenettes, and more amply appointed suites, but one thing

remains constant: the bliss of bedding down to the sounds of the surf lapping on the shore.

Style 7, Atmosphere 8, Location 8

Chateau Marmont, 8221 W Sunset Blvd (Laurel Canyon), West Hollywood
Tel: 323 656 1010   www.chateaumarmont.com
Rates: $370–3,500

"If you must get in trouble," advised Harry Cohn, the notorious head of Columbia Pictures, "do it at the Chateau Marmont." Perched majestically in the Hollywood hillside where the Sunset Strip and Laurel Canyon converge, since 1927 the Chateau has been the epitome of mystique, mojo, and mayhem (Gable and Harlow trysted, Morrison dangled from a drainpipe, Zeppelin rode motorcycles through the lobby, Belushi OD'ed, and Lohan relaxed post-rehab amid its hallowed halls). Eccentric and elegant, zealously

mindful of both its patrons' privacy and their urge to be seen, gloriously glamorous yet tolerant of its guests' naughtier proclivities (mostly... Britney Spears was booted once), it's the ultimate Hollywood hedonist's hotel. Trouble beckons.

Style 9, Atmosphere 9/10, Location 9

Farmer's Daughter Hotel, 115 S Fairfax Ave (3rd St), West Hollywood
Tel: 323 937 3930 www.farmersdaughterhotel.com
Rates: $179–275

Hankerin' for a funky, economical inn experience? A roll in the hay with Farmer's Daughter might make your cock crow. Once a dilapidated motel, it's been remade into a faux-countrified, sexed-up hipster haven – denim bedspreads, sunflowers, and cowskin rugs prevail – for the budget-boutique

set eschewing big-chain banality. It hosts its own kooky lounge, Tart, lies across the street from the famed Farmer's Market and The Grove shopping center, and for those coming on down to The Price Is Right tapings, it's so close you can practically hear the Plinko chips dropping. Like its pigtailed namesake, it's a love-it-or-leave-it locale, so if the Daisy Dukes fit…

Style 7, Atmosphere 6, Location 7

Four Seasons Hotel, 300 S Doheny Drive (3rd St), Beverly Hills
Tel: 310 273 2222   www.fourseasons.com/losangeles
Rates: $435–5,000

It's all about the experience. While not quite as lavish as some of its sister

properties, this always-bustling high-rise hotel lives up to its venerated brand by delivering exemplary service, high-end amenities (oh, those specially designed Serta beds!), and an abundance of understated elegance. Its location on the LA/Beverly Hills border can't be beat, set away from the throngs yet sublimely adjacent to luxurious 90210, trendy Robertson Boulevard, and West Hollywood's party playgrounds. A central gathering spot for showbiz types and a prime press junket locale, you won't spend much time in the lobby, the chummy cocktail bar, or even the hallways outside your suite without catching a glimpse of a major star or two.

Style 7, Atmosphere 8, Location 9

Hollywood Roosevelt Hotel, 7000 Hollywood Blvd (Orange), Hollywood

Tel: 323 466 7000 www.hollywoodroosevelt.com
Rates: $209–6,000

This city loves a comeback: after 80 years reigning over Hollywood Boulevard, falling in and out of favor, the Roosevelt – the site of the very

first Oscars – is hip, hot, and haute all over again, offering an unequaled mix of classic charms (the penthouse suite where Gable and Lombard got it on, or the soon to be revamped Cinegrill music lounge) and of-the-moment excitement (in-house hotspots Teddy's, the poolside Tropicana Bar and Dakota steakhouse). Recast inside
by designer Dodd Mitchell into a moody, minimalist den for the young, pretty, and privileged, it nevertheless retains haunting echoes of its storied past: Montgomery Clift's ghost is said to roam his ninth-floor suite, and check your look in the full-length mirror in the lobby by the elevator that once adorned Marilyn Monroe's room: her spirit just might look back.

Style 9, Atmosphere 9, Location 9

Hotel Angeleno, 170 N Church Lane (Sunset), Brentwood

Tel: 310 476 6411 www.hotelangeleno.com
Rates: $209–369

This new-ish property from hoteliers Joie de Vivre is a distinct up-and-comer after refitting a former Holiday Inn built in a far-out Space Age circular tower motif into a W-style bastion of modern luxury and contemporary

cool. Overlooking the oft-bumper-to-bumper 405 Freeway at the crossroads of tony Brentwood and billionaire-y Bel-Air, the Angeleno offers spectacular views of the region – especially the panorama at the intimate rooftop lounge West – and makes for an easy stop-off to the nearby must-visit Getty Center. "It's all about the bed" is the mantra there, delivering a decadent mattress and bedding experience. The traffic din detracts sometimes, but hey, better up here than down there.

Style 8, Atmosphere 8, Location 8

Hotel Bel-Air, 701 Stone Canyon Rd (Tortuoso), Bel Air

Tel: 310 472 1211 www.hotelbelair.com
Rates: $395–4,000

If there is one elite hotel experience in the area that truly deserves the description 'magical' it belongs to this sublime five-star destination, easily the most enchanting and exquisite accommodations in town. Stepping across

the quaint stone bridge that spans the swan-filled lake is like crossing an otherworldly portal into a spellbinding alternate universe – there's nothing 'LA' about it, except for the sunshine, the service, and the starry clientele (oh, and the sky-high prices). Filling about a dozen lushly landscaped acres in the heart of the ultra-exclusive community, the serene Spanish Colonial-style setting is rapturously rarefied and resoundingly romantic.

Style 9, Atmosphere 9, Location 8

The Huntley Hotel, 1111 Second Street (California Ave), Santa Monica,
Tel: 310 394 5454 www.thehuntleyhotel.com
Rates: $469–1,900

Just a block from the beach or the bustle of Santa Monica's Third Street Promenade and awash with the scent of jasmine candles, the recently beau-

tified Huntley offers California-dreamy creamy-white scenes ranging from bucolic to boisterous. The lobby is all artsy-cool urban oasis, with over-sized leather armchairs, eclectic furnishings, exotic artwork, refined woods, and an abundance of orchids – and yes, those are white lacquered piranhas on the wall. The rooms boast a mod retro mix of vintage-inspired appointments and caramel suede headboards, and the Huntley's crowning achievement is the always-hip-deep-in-hipsters Penthouse lounge, where you must decide which is more gorgeous: the panoramic Pacific views or the ethereal design scheme.

Style 9/10, Atmosphere 9, Location 8

London West Hollywood, 1020 N San Vicente Blvd (Sunset), West Hollywood

Tel: 866 282 4560 www.thelondonwesthollywood.com
Rates: $249–1,200

The newly opened London West Hollywood, a sister property to the NYC outpost and similarly including the Hell's Kitchen chef Gordon Ramsay's eponymous outpost. The retro and fabulous chic stylings of Brit designer

David Collins, who has decided to bring just a little bit of the English countryside to glam West Hollywood; check out the terribly English ornamental terraces complete with 'bulldog' topiary. Weathered timbers, new-style chintz and industrial 'luxe' meet in an ambitious and deeply sexy interior. The rooftop pool and spa attract the starlets by the dozen and the Cocktail Bar is all about sheer indulgence. To round off the anglophile theme posh British concierge service Quintessentially man the desks to bring you your heart's desires.

Style 9, Atmosphere 9, Location 9

Maison 140, 140 Lasky Drive (Santa Monica), Beverly Hills

Tel: 800 670 6182 www.maison140beverlyhills.com
Rates: $165–279

Parisian pied-a-terre meets the Asian aesthetic as envisioned by interior designer Kelly Wearstler in Beverly Hills' premiere boutique hotel, tucked away on a quiet side street bridging the business and residential districts.

Intimate, intricate, enticing, exotic, dark, dramatic, campy, chic – Maison 140 inspires an array of adjectives most luxury accommodations don't, and provides all of the requisite amenities. Each of the 43 rooms has its own distinct, one-of-a-kind French-meets-Far-East flair, with custom-designed furniture and eclectic antiquities, and the staff continues to earn the highest marks for their dedication to fulfilling one's every whim. And even though it doesn't offer its own poolside scene, guests are allowed to take a dip at sister property the Avalon just a quick jaunt away.

Style 9, Atmosphere 8, Location 8

Malibu Beach Inn, 22878 Pacific Coast Highway (Sweetwater Canyon), Malibu
Tel: 310 456 6444 www.malibubeachinn.com
Rates: $325–975

Media mogul David Geffen's 47-room inn has undergone multimillion-dollar renovations that have only upgraded its considerable Carbon Beach cachet with a masculine-mellow, surf-chic design scheme. Though it still seems a bit like a work in progress – the rooms and furnishings don't quite equal loftier expectations – aesthetic touches like the hand-painted bath tiles, private balconies, high-tech amenities, and photrealisitic artwork by Glenn Ness, as well as its proximity to Pepperdine University, the Malibu Country Mart, and historic Adamson House, are a plus. But what you're really shelling out serious clams for here is the shoreline steps away – though technically the highly coveted stretch is a public beach, non-guests pay $75 daily for access at

the inn's Carbon Beach Club.

Style 7, Atmosphere 7, Location 9

The Mondrian, 8440 W Sunset Blvd (Olive Drive), West Hollywood

Tel: 323 650 8999 www.mondrianhotel.com
Rates: $310–2,500

The epicenter of all things cool after its dramatic 90s debut, hotelier Ian Schrager's ultra-modern, ultra-minimalist Sunset Strip hotspot remains a central gathering place for the most beautiful of beautiful people – and especially the LA equivalent of the bridge-and-tunnelers from the Valley and the OC hoping to rub elbows with them at its sexy Skybar and restaurant Asia de Cuba; the people-watching, from Paris Hilton to posers, is as eye-

popping as the city view. We wonder what designer Philippe Starck has up his sleeve for the pending redesign, but the current all-white color scheme – from the sweepingly curtained lobby down to staff uniforms – is all-pervasive pearly, evoking Heaven's hotel – if Heaven's denizens wore little black Bebe dresses and Ed Hardy tees.

Style 8, Atmosphere 7, Location 7

The Mosaic Hotel, 125 S. Spalding Drive (Wilshire), Beverly Hills

Tel: 310 278 0303   www.mosaichotel.com
Rates: $225–800

This cheery, daffodil-yellow boutique hotel is squeal-inducing for the *Sex and the City*-style gal on holiday in BevHills. Tucked discreetly away on a side street, the 49-room Mosaic is understated in its elegance, and just a quick trot (in stylish but comfy Manolos, natch) away from the chic clotheshorse's

paradise that is 90210. After toting back bags from Saks, Neiman's, and Rodeo Drive, she can shop-detox by the intimate, purple-illuminated pool before grabbing a signature sake martini amid the mosaic-tiled walls of the cozy cocktail lounge, maybe chatted up by one of the cute, hip agent/manager/producer-types at the bar. After that? Well, the rooms boast fabulous Frette bedding, and it isn't always just about a good night's sleep...

Style 9, Atmosphere 7, Location 8

The Peninsula Beverly Hills, 9882 S Santa Monica Blvd (Lasky), Beverly Hills

Tel: 310 551 2888 www.beverlyhills.peninsula.com
Rates: $325–6,000

Known as the ultimate private hideaway for the high-powered and high-profile – those truly wishing not to be seen, whether conducting clandestine business in classy environs or even laying low following a little nip/tuck – the Peninsula serves sophisticated European formality in high style, with one of

the most accommodating staffs imaginable. Everything's exquisitely tasteful, tony, and, when necessary, discreet, from the English high tea in the Living Room to the creative spa services to the world-class Belvedere restaurant, and at night the Club Bar is a dealmaker's dream den, whether closing a three-picture pact or an assignation with one of the lovelies lining the room.

Style 8, Atmosphere 8, Location 8

Raffles L'Ermitage, 9291 Burton Way (Foothill), Beverly Hills,

Tel: 800 800 2113 www.beverlyhills.raffles.com
Rates: $435–6,400

L'Ermitage has earned five-star and five-diamond rating for eight years running, and just about every other top accolade offered – what else do you need to know? Here's a few things: its Beverly Hills berth is close to the city's action (that's shopping and dining) but just out of the way enough for a laid-back, low-profile escape; its modern, Asian-by-way-of-Scandinavian

design scheme is opulent without being overwhelming; the mega-luxe rooms are as high-tech as can be imagined, and guests are given customized stationery and business cards. Need even more enticement? Brad Pitt's been known to hang at the lobby Writer's Bar, where the walls are lined with original manuscripts and screenplays from acclaimed authors.

Style 8, Atmosphere 8, Location 7

The Shade Hotel, 1221 N Valley Drive (Manhattan Beach) Manhattan Beach
Tel: 310 546 4995 www.shadehotel.com
Rates: $180–895

Precious few lodgings outside LA's mainstream centers garner much notice – especially if brand new with no big corporate name – but Manhattan

Beach's 38-room boutique hotel Shade basked in the limelight since day one, earning raves for bringing a perfect blend of sand-n-surf sensibility, maritime chic, and all-around cool to the coastal community's increasingly hip center. The Zinc lounge is such a local hotspot the hotel often opens the rooftop Skydeck with its views of Catalina to handle the overflow. The body-contouring Tempur-Pedic beds and pillows thrill some and throw some, but other abundant pleasures include Cyclone fireplaces, Sanijet spa tubs for two, and guests are aglow over the modifiable multicolored mood lighting that could only be called 'chromatherapy.'

Style 9, Atmosphere 7, Location 6

Shutters on the Beach, 1 Pico Blvd (Appian), Santa Monica
Tel: 310 450 0030   www.shuttersonthebeach.com
Rates: $480–3,500

So New England in its design you almost expect to spot a salty seafarer toting a netfull of freshly caught crabs through its long, luxuriant lobby, but it's really Californian through and through. Though it debuted in 1993, Shutters

feels timeless, a bucolic beach-house resort mere steps from Pacific and ideally situated for anything from shopping on Third Street Promenade, traipsing to the nearby Santa Monica Pier or strolling the shoreline down to funky Venice Beach. Casual yet chic and oh-so-serene, it's also an idyllic site for romantic seaside weddings, especially if the bride and groom want to feel sand between their toes moments after the "I Dos."

Style 7, Atmosphere 8, Location 9

The Standard Downtown, 550 S Flower St (W 6th St), Downtown

Tel: 213 892 8080 www.standardhotels.com/los-angeles
Rates: $99–1,150

Talk about setting the standard: Andre Balzas' retro-futuristic downtown venture in a former oil company building struck such a gusher of success

after its launch in 2001, it spearheaded the re-hip-ification of the once-down-trodden Downtown dis-trict. And, oh, how very hip and now it is – think of it as the anti-Biltmore. Everything from the upside-down signage to funky modernist rooms that come in 'Huge,' 'Gigantic,' 'Humongous,' and 'Wow!' sizes to the high-energy Hollywoodite scene that always has the 12th floor Rooftop Bar hopping with hottie's screams, "This ain't your daddy's luxury hotel!"

(though even Dad might enjoy an eyeful of the slinky scenemakers on parade).

Style 7, Atmosphere 8, Location 7

Sunset Marquis Hotel, 1200 N. Alta Loma Road, West Hollywood

Tel: 310 657 1333 www.sunsetmarquishotel.com
Rates: $300–7,000

Launched in 1963 as the Hyatt House a.k.a. the 'Riot House,' the lodging of choice for the rambunctiously rowdy Rock God scene – Led Zeppelin, the

Rolling Stones, U2, you name it, they slept it off here (the hotel even boasts an on-site recording facility) – it's been reborn as a study in ultra-cool con-tradictions. Entering from the Sunset Strip's all-day din, the tranquility of three Eden-esque acres of lush tropical grounds takes one aback. Throughout the property, the clichéd conventioneer décor has finally been chucked in favor of clean yet edgy modern elegance. So serene, until sun-down, when today's rockers, rappers, and scenesters rise, flocking to the in-house Whiskey Bar (often piping in those newly -laid tracks) for after-dark dallying that'd make Keith Moon proud.

Style 8, Atmosphere 8, Location 7

Viceroy Santa Monica, 1819 Ocean Avenue, Santa Monica,
Tel: 310 260 7500 www.viceroysantamonica.com
Rates: $469–1,500

How is this place both 'cosmopolitan' and 'shagadelic' simultaneously? Much credit goes to Kelly Wearstler's quirky design, which somehow marries veddy colonial British formality with a mad Mod 60s sensibility, united in an unexpected yet alluring color scheme of parrot green, driftwood gray, and wavecrest white – it's as pleasing to gaze at as it is to stay there. Everything flows fluidly into the next eye-catching attraction, from the minimalist front desk to the chic Cameo Bar (named for the oversized brooch dominating the lobby wall) into china-lined Whist restaurant out onto the posh pool and cabanas and back in again. No wonder it serves as a hotbed for hip locals seeking a cosmo, a shag, or both – they came to the right place.

Style 8, Atmosphere 8, Location 8

W Hotel, 930 Hilgard Ave (Le Conte), Westwood

Tel: 310 208 8765 www.starwoodhotels.com
Rates: $279–3,000

Only Queer Eye's Thom Filica could sum up his W design scheme so color-
fully: "Babe Paley meets Neutra." That's the ambiance at this suite-only hotel

in the tree-lined neighborhood alongside UCLA – modernist chic for the
country club cabana set. There's an array of wonders – the astonishingly
expansive suites, the only Bliss spa in Southern California, the sofa-appoint-
ed, waterfall-flowing outdoor pool area The Backyard, the minimalist dining
room NineThirty and the lengthy cocktail lounge Whiskey Blue, where cou-
tured coeds congregate to play sophisticate. Everything here seems over-

sized, in the best possible way, allowing for a relaxed airiness that keeps some of the super-sleek trappings of this former college dormitory from feeling too cool for school.

Style 8, Atmosphere 7, Location 7

Zen Retreats,
Tel: 323 962 0270 www.zen-retreats.com
Rates: $250–500

Nestled away in the hills underneath the Hollywood sign is the perfect alternative for those wanting to escape the confines of a hotel and make

their own way in LA. Three bijou, Japanese-inspired apartments (a studio, a one bed and a two bed) are hidden away behind a tall bamboo fence. Inside, the rooms are pure zen minimalism, unfussy, uncluttered and supremely comfortable, blended with all the modern conveniences a guest could want. In Koi (the one bed) there is a roaring gas fire in the bathroom to enjoy stretched out in the sunken tub, while an expansive balcony gives views out over Los Feliz, towards Downtown. Staying here you will need a car, but you are close enough to the freeway, Hollywood and West Hollywood to be within 10 minutes drive of all the action. For those who want to really play the LA part, the owner's dog wanders around nonchantly and is amenable to going for walks in the local park.

Style 8, Atmosphere 8, Location 7

Notes & Updates

Notes & Updates

eat...

It's often said that you are what you eat. Well, in this town, where you eat is pretty darn telling, too. With so much wealth, power, and personality going on among the LA population, its restaurants are anything but ordinary. The population is incredibly diverse, so you can have culinary adventures every night of the week if you'd care to – Korean barbecue, Oaxacan delights, spectacular sushi, and so on. Thanks to the city's sunny, fair climate and ideal location, fish and produce are absolutely divine, and most chefs keep their menus malleable to accommodate fresh ingredients that become available at the farmer's market. Dining out is never dull, and if you land in the right place at the right time, you never know who you might be seated next to. (Mariah Carey? John Stewart? La Toya Jackson? Jackie Collins?)

Then there are the celebrity chefs – Wolfgang Puck, David Myers, Joachim Splichal, Gordon Ramsay (below), Nancy Silverton, Kerry Simon, Mario Batali, Eric Greenspan, etc. Los Angeles is the perfect playground for a world-class chef to show off to an influential, appreciative audience. With so many studio executives, talent agents, publicists, stylists, directors, screenwriters, and movie stars bopping around town, there is never a shortage of big personalities willing to spend big money on an impressive meal. Knowing this, these big culinary

guns do their darndest to uphold the highest standards of quality and creativity… and perhaps to show one another up now and again.

Star chef or no star chef, there's great food to be found all over town. You have no excuse for settling on mediocre meals while you're here. In LA, people love to act like they know the 'in' spots, so you're likely to have plenty of choices.

Each neighborhood has its own style and vibe, and their eateries tend to reflect the local population. In Venice and Santa Monica, it's all about post-beach pleasures. In WeHo and Hollywood, maybe you're looking for a bit of sex appeal and star power. In Beverly Hills, you'll find plenty of lovely luxuries. Silver Lake and Los Feliz – 'cutting edge' and 'cool' are the buzzwords there.

It was extraordinarily difficult choosing the right restaurants for this guide… LA has such a bounty of spectacular food, and there are hundreds of institutions that deserve your consideration… Joan's on Third (8350 Third Street between La Cienega and Fairfax) is hugely popular, and we just love Joan. The Palm on Santa Monica (9001 Santa Monica Blvd) is a classic LA experience, with gargantuan steaks and caricatures of its more notable diners. Asia de Cuba (8440 Sunset Blvd) is a sexy scene at the Mondrian hotel, where the fab fusion fare draws in glittering guests. The notorious celeb scene at Mr. Chow's (344 N. Camden Dr) never fails to impress. And Kerry Simon's Simon LA (8555 Beverly Blvd) at the Sofitel hotel is impossibly cool.

So, come with an open mind… Try new flavors, give the unusual a chance to win you over. Isn't that what this city is all about?

Our top ten restaurants in Los Angeles are:
1. Sona
2. Spago
3. A.O.C.
4. Gordon Ramsay at the London
5. Providence
6. Osteria Mozza
7. Melisse
8. Ortolan
9. Cut
10. Campanile

Our top five restaurants for food are:
1. Sona
2. Osteria Mozza
3. Campanile
4. Melisse
5. A.O.C.

Our top five restaurants for service are:
1. Spago
2. Gordon Ramsay at the London
3. Comme Ca
4. All'Angelo
5. Belvedere

Our top five restaurants for atmosphere are:
1. Via Veneto
2. Jar
3. Nobu Los Angeles
4. Providence
5. Comme Ca

A.O.C., 8022 W 3rd Street (Crescent Heights), Hollywood

Tel: 323 653 6359   www.aocwinebar.com
Open: daily, 6pm (5.30pm Sat/Sun)–11pm (10pm Sun) $65
Mediterranean

Even the smallest bites yield big reactions at this sophisticated, wine-focused Mediterranean spot at the intersection of W 3rd and Crescent Heights. In

keeping with its name – short for *appellation d'origine controlle*, the French system of labeling wine – oenophiles delight at the lengthy and impressive wine list, not to mention the well-informed suggestions of the attractive wait staff. Charcuterie and fine cheese aficionados will be particularly pleased, as will anyone with an affinity for brave flavor combos, for which chef Suzanne Goin has a particular knack. Just a taste: Dungeness crab salad with corn pancakes, *gnocchi* with lobster and *pancetta*, and heavenly *brioche* with *prosciutto*, gruyére, and egg from the

wood-burning oven. Plan on ordering about three small plates per person, and place your implicit trust in the kitchen.

Food 9, Service 9, Atmosphere 9

All'Angelo, 7166 Melrose Ave (La Brea), Hollywood,

Tel: 323 933 9540   www.allangelo.com
Open: noon–2.30pm, 6–10.30pm. Closed Sat lunch and Sun. $63
Italian

Fans of fine Italian fare need look no further than this wonderfully authentic eatery from Valentino and Il Drago alum Stefano Ongaro, who use any and every opportunity to appeal to their guests' finer sensibilities, be it with the

subdued and stylish décor (sconces, hand-blown glass, soothing yellow walls) or the celebrated cuisine of executive chef Mirko Paderno, who reigned supreme at Dolce. Paderno is truly gifted, able to amp up Italian staples with refined bursts of flavor – think delicate and fragrant risotto, a soul-satisfying selection of pastas, perfectly prepared whole fish, hearty lamb or pork chops, and so on. A seven course tasting menu goes for $95, and is a grand way to celebrate in style. Do take advantage of the wine and dine *prix fixe* for $39, Monday through Thursday… It's too satisfying a deal to pass up.

Food 8, Service 8, Atmosphere 8

Animal, 435 N Fairfax Ave (Rosewood), West Hollywood

Tel: 323 782 9225   www.animalrestaurant.com
Open: daily, 6–11pm (2am Fri/Sat) $64
Modern American

Chefs Jon Shook and Vinnie Ditolo don't pull punches when it comes to satisfying carnivorous cravings. Shook and Ditolo are a manly catering duo dubbed the 'Food Dudes,' and their palate-cosseting ways have won them plenty of fans in recent years. For this new spot they've opted to do away with too much pomp and circumstance in terms of décor – don't look for a sign, or overdone details… just a wall-length bench and inviting copper bar. Instead, they explore the potent possibilities of seasonal ingredients and marvelous meat with inspired, weekly-changing menus. Indeed, as its name suggests, this is not a vegetarian paradise… but if you're a fan of pork in all its permutations, get thee there. Much has been made of the bacon-

enhanced chocolate for dessert... Don't be afraid to admit that you're just
a little bit curious.

Food 9, Service 8, Atmosphere 7

Belvedere, The Peninsula, 9882 Santa Monica Blvd (Lasky), Beverly Hills
Tel: 310 551 2888   www.beverlyhills.peninsula.com
Open: 6.30am–10.30pm Mon–Sat; 11am–2.30pm, 6–10.30pm Sun $75
Modern American

When you feel like you've earned a ritzy, glitzy meal, and your wallet can
withstand a significant hit, indulge in the modern American fare of the
Peninsula hotel's celebrated eatery. This refined shrine to good gastronomy
works with the hotel's highbrow sensibilities and capitalizes on the freshest

Cali flavors, hitting the right notes for a privacy-seeking (meaning: boldfaced and powerful) clientele night after day after night. Decadent comforts like local foie gras, mac n' cheese with Taleggio cheese and black truffles, or artichokes and Dungeness crab set the tone before the amped-up classic entrees appear — think a sizzling 18-ounce Kansas City strip steak, a perfectly prepared Maine lobster, and even a tofu tasting with bok choi, mushrooms, and glass noodles. When the glorious SoCal sun in shining — and often it is — snag a seat on the landscaped patio… It's another world.

Food 8, Service 9, Atmosphere 8

BLD, 7450 Beverly Blvd (Vista), Mid-Wilshire
Tel: 323 930 9744 www.bldrestaurant.com
Open: daily, 8am–11pm $50
American

Standing for 'breakfast, lunch, dinner,' this much loved, laidback Mid-Wilshire offering possesses the qualities of our favorite brand of Angeleno: sexy yet never fussy, sophisticated yet uncomplicated, and ultimately easy to love for its great taste and friendliness. We'll take a long lunch here any day, splitting

the myriad all-American comforts — delicately realized pastas, prime burger made with Wagyu beef, beautiful desserts that pack a punch — over a well-selected bottle of wine.

(Though if you and your companion's wine tastes differ, their by-the-glass offerings are impressive.) And when we've been out 'til the wee hours, crawling into a chair within this gentle sunny environment while servers offer French press coffee and ricotta pancakes is a surefire hangover remedy. If you're a staunch vegan, you'll be pleasantly surprised by their flavorful take on creature-free grub.

Food 9, Service 7, Atmosphere 7

Café Stella, 3932 W Sunset Blvd (Sanborn), Silver Lake
Tel: 323 666 0265
Open: daily, 6–11pm (10pm Sun) $60
French bistro

This hip, heavenly bistro at Sunset Junction (the corner of Sanborn Avenue) attracts Silverlake and Los Feliz tastemakers with its spot-on classic French fare, romantic atmosphere, and funky yet pulled-together wait staff. Go for

the sure-bets like *steak au poivre* and *escargots*, though don't overlook the Niman Ranch pork chop, braised short ribs, or sautéed salmon with mustard and herb butter.

Desserts go beyond satisfying, if you have room enough for them at the end of your sumptuous first courses. It's rare that there's a spare table waiting for you, so make your reservations in advance. Star-gazers and third-daters, take note: there's a dreamy, candlelit patio to rival any in the city. Once through, the strolling at Sunset Junction is entertaining – as is the leather apparel and fetish store across the street.

Food 8, Service 8, Atmosphere 8

Campanile, 624 S. La Brea Avenue (6th), Miracle Mile

Tel: 323 938 1447 www.campanilerestaurant.com

Open: 11.30am (9.30am Sat/Sun)–2.30pm (1.30pm Sat/Sun), 6pm (5.30pm Thurs–Sat)–10pm (11pm Thurs–Sat) $50

Californian/French

All of your favorite flavors are taken to exquisite territory at chef-owner Mark Peel's French-California gastro-land, located in the former offices of film legend Charlie Chaplin. Like Chaplin's movies, you'll be struck silent by

the fine, rustic fare coming from the open kitchen... There will inevitably come a point, about two minutes into the sizable appetizers, that reverential chewing and savoring will replace chit-chatting, and such interludes will continue throughout the remainder of the evening, all the way to the blueberry-brown butter tart and profiteroles. Peel obviously takes great pride and pleasure in crafting his menu, and doesn't joke around when it comes to freshness. Baked goods hail all the way from next door, where Peel's LA Brea Bakery fires up heavenly bread – just try and beat those baguettes and batards – and his dishes come alive with color and taste, thanks to top market produce and meats. We'll go for his grilled big-eye tuna or pan-roasted black cod any day, though sometime we must indulge in that unforgettable rosemary-charred baby lamb or decadent grilled Wagyu beef tri-tip. Reserve for a Thursday to try any number of specialty grilled cheeses. Winning wines, too.

Food 9, Service 9, Atmosphere 9

Catch, Hotel Casa Del Mar, 1910 Ocean Way (Pico), Santa Monica

Tel: 310 581 7714 www.hotelcasadelmar.com
Open: daily, 11.30am–3pm, 6–10pm $80
French/American seafood

Just a flip and a flop from the breathtaking Pacific shore, this elegant seafood destination is what Santa Monica style is all about – lush relaxation, refined yet unfussy tastes, and simple aesthetic beauty. Its floor-to-ceiling windows allow diners to delight in the crashing waves while luxuriating in plush white

banquettes or deep cushioned chairs. Handsome executive chef Michael Reardon is no slouch, and his artful culinary presentations are as easy to stare at as they are to devour. Reardon loves to capitalize on farmer's market freshness, as is evidenced by the artful salads and veggie dishes, while oceanic offerings truly do rule the day. It's easy to just fill up on the out-of-this-world *crudo* and sushi rolls, but you'd be missing out on sublime grilled branzino, Alaskan halibut with zucchini and squash blossoms, and light handmade ravioli Bolognese.

Food 8, Service 9, Atmosphere 9

Cheebo, 7533 W Sunset Blvd (Gardner), Hollywood

Tel: 323 850 7070 www.cheebo.com
Open: daily, 8am (11am Mon/Tues)–11.30pm (12.30am Fri/Sat) $35
Italian–American

Casually cool, as organic as possible, and delicious as can be, this tangerine-

tinted charmer on Sunset – right near the legendary Guitar Center – has no shortage of fans, be they lunching execs from Paramount, jeans-clad screenwriters meeting with their potential unknown stars, or shaggy-haired locals. They all jones for the hard-to-beat Cheebo chop salad (organic greens tossed with morsels of chicken, salami, *garbanzo* beans, *provolone*, and tomatoes) or the homemade-sausage and fennel pizza, served by the foot. Display your artistic talents with the provided crayons on the paper-topped tables, but be sure not to spill any fresh-squeezed juice, spot-on wine, or delish bloody Mary (the Cheeb-o-Mary) on your stellar creation. If you're not going the way of pizza (or even if you are!) start with the Cheebread, addictive flatbread with fragrant rosemary or drizzled in garlic and extra virgin olive oil.

Food 8, Service 7, Atmosphere 7

Citrus at Social, 6525 Sunset Blvd (Schrader), Hollywood
Tel: 323 337 9797 www.chinagrillmgt.com
Open: daily, 6–11pm (midnight Thurs–Sat) $76
Californian/French

Superchef Michel Richard – who made waves in town 20 years ago with the original Citrus on Melrose – isn't one to play around. When it comes to conceiving and executing award-winning dining establishments, he has his skilled hands in every element, and this stylish offering at hopping nightclub Social – located in the Hollywood Athletic Club building – is proof. This time around, he teamed with big-thinking restaurateur/nightlife impresario Jeffrey Chodorow, and the results are both super stylish and wildly popular. Richard

brings great vision and innovation to the sexy Cal-French menu, highlights of which include cuttlefish *carbonara*, the 72-hour short ribs, a lovely lobster burger, and the 'duck, duck, orange.' (See there… Richard is a world-class chef, but he insists on fun. That translates to the crowd, and keeps them coming back.) Desserts are kind of required… The Kit Kat Bar with sauce Noisette, hails from Richard's Washington, D.C. sensation Citronelle, and the pastries are out of this world. Then, shake off the calories on the dance floor!

Food 8, Service 8, Atmosphere 9

Cobras & Matadors 7615 W Beverly Blvd (Curson), West Hollywood
Tel: 323 932 6178
Open: daily, 5–11pm (midnight Fri/Sat) $42
Spanish/Tapas

Reigning supreme among the designer denim-and-blazer crowd, these tempting *tapas* mainstays are all about the passion and flavors of Spain. The young and beautiful scenesters who keep these small rooms a-buzz know they'll be walking into an agreeable scene any day of the week, and the sizzling, sharable small plates keep the dynamic convivially communal. Our favorites include the cured *jamón* with aged goat cheese, sugar *chile* prawns, barbecued skirt steak marinated in orange juice, and salt cod cakes. The bacon-wrapped shrimp are no joke, and you can always just opt for the platters of Spanish cheeses or charcuterie. There is a sizable Spanish wine list, including many by the glass, though there is no corkage fee if you bring your

own vino. There is a second outpost at 4655 Hollywood Blvd (Vermont), Los Feliz; tel: 323 669 3922.

Food 8, Service 7, Atmosphere 8

Comme Ça, 8479 Melrose Avenue (La Cienega), West Hollywood,

Tel: 323 782 1104 www.commecarestaurant.com

Open: 11.30am–2.30pm, 5–11pm (midnight Fri/Sat). Closed Sun lunch. $78

French

Perhaps our favorite chef in all of Lalaland, David Myers – whose bakery Boule is plucked down from the heavens – has been amazing the masses with his inventive and heartfelt offerings at Sona for years. More recently, this power bistro on Melrose has been the reservation of choice for indus-

try bigwigs, food snobs, and all those folks who just have to be around greatness. Cool, comforting, cozy, creative… Myers doesn't try and reinvent the wheel. Rather, he takes those sumptuous Parisian tastes and manipulates them masterfully. Your palate isn't being tricked, it's being romanced. As logic would dictate, the wine list is winning and wonderful, with 20-plus by-the-glass options (or bring your own, knowing there's a $25 corkage fee). The cocktails are some of the coolest in town. Oh yes, then there's the food… *Coq au vin*, *boeuf Bourguignon*, *bouillabaisse*, and a dreamy, concise take on *steak frites* that you'll dream about a few months later.

Food 9, Service 9, Atmosphere 8

Crustacean, 9646 S Santa Monica Blvd (Bedford), Beverly Hills

Tel: 310 205 8990   www.anfamily.com
Open: 11.30am–2.30pm, 5.30–10.30pm (11.30pm Fri) Mon–Fri;
5.30–11.30pm Sat $72
European/Vietnamese

A perennially hot scene for over a decade, this wining Euro-Vietnamese eatery is a haven for the rich, powerful, picky, and privileged. Owned by the

iconic An family – their restaurants are pure gold here and in San Francisco – its tranquil bi-level environment was inspired by their former French Colonial estate, located in Hanoi, and features a sparkling koi stream, an indoor fountain, and antiques galore. (Don't you just love this town?) But don't think it's all fuss and no sub-stance… The kitchen is adept and has many tricks to unfurl. The

famous garlic noodles and whole cracked crab are hard to argue with, but anything you pick will most likely please you. Some sure winners: the vegetable-laden Buddha's Delight, the dumpling trio with tamarind ginger balsamic sauce, the secret-recipe 'drunken crab,' and ponzu glazed filet mignon. Conclude with the Eurasian fritters… they're good stuff.

Food 9, Service 7, Atmosphere 8

Cut, 9500 Wilshire Blvd (Rodeo), Beverly Hills
Tel: 310 275 5200 www.fourseasons.com/beverlywilshire
Open: 5.30–10.30pm Mon–Sat $76
Steak

Few names resonate as deeply in the hearts and stomachs of LA foodies as Wolfgang Puck. The Cali cuisine legend has outdone himself here at the ritzy Beverly Wilshire hotel, where the fare is as sumptuous as the aesthetic is

spare. Richard Meier's placid, all-white design sets a chic, clean stage for Puck to perform, and perform her does… All the time-honored steakhouse classics are turned up a notch: Maryland blue crab and Louisiana shrimp cocktail, herbed fries, creamed spinach with organic fried egg, potato *tarte tatin*… and then, the marvelous meat, grilled over hardwood and charcoal, then finished off by a 1,200 degree broiler. Be it genuine Japanese Wagyu beef filet mignon, USDA prime porterhouse, or a 35-day aged Nebraska corn-fed rib-eye, carnivores will have plenty to dream about.

Food 9, Service 8, Atmosphere 8

Dominick's, 8715 Beverly Blvd (Sherbourne), West Hollywood,

Tel: 310 652 2335 www.dominicksrestaurant.com

Open: daily, 6–11pm $58

Italian

The spirit of the Rat Pack permeates this wholly agreeable Italian standout, which was frequented by Sinatra and pals back in their heyday. The current owners – Walter Ebbink and the chef, Brandon Boudet – painstakingly

restored its charms a few years back and have enjoyed a seal of approval from local foodies and luminaries. Its draws: Boudet's reverential takes on Italian classics, a sexy wine list with selections that range from tried-and-true to hard-to-find, a genial staff, involved management, and a cool, romantic setting that will make you wonder if you haven't been transported to New York's Mulberry Street. Indeed, the white-tile floors and plush red booths are classic Little Italy, though the bar scene is distinctly modern, and the brick patio ensconced by a working herb garden is out of a fairy tale. For a homey slice of fun, do try the $15 three-course, family-style Italian meal supper every Sunday, which offers the house wine, Dago Red, for $10 per bottle. Eastsiders are rejoicing, too… The restaurant's little bro, Little Dom's, is open on Hillhurst in Los Feliz.

Food 8, Service 8, Atmosphere 9

Gordon Ramsay, The London West Hollywood, 1020 N. San Vicente Blvd (Sunset), West Hollywood,

Tel: 310 358 7788   www.thelondonwesthollywood.com
Open: daily, 6.30am–10.30am, noon–3pm, 5–10.30pm $82
Modern eclectic

You've probably watched Gordon Ramsay throw a hot-headed fit on television, reducing some poor chefling to tears or infuriating a restaurant owner with uncensored criticism. Or perhaps you've been on the east coast and scored a table at the London's Manhattan outpost. Whatever you think about his personality, you have to admit that the guy knows what he's talk-

ing about. Ramsay oversees every morsel at the spectacular London – located in the former Bel Age space – and pulls many a trick out of his sleeve. All you and your taste buds need do is relax into the funky pastel environment (courtesy of Brit designer David Collins), allow the knowledgeable wait staff to guide you through the grand menu, and let the night take you away. Just a sampling: pressed Hudson Valley foie gras tapioca, roasted monkfish tail with fennel hearts and baby root veggies, Colorado lamb loin with perfectly braised shank, and a delicate pineapple soufflé with Thai curry ice cream and toasted coconut.

Food 9, Service 8, Atmosphere 8

Grace, 7360 Beverly Blvd (Fuller), West Hollywood

Tel: 323 934 4400   www.gracerestaurant.com
Open: 6–10.30pm (11pm Sat, 10pm Sun). Closed Mondays. $90
Modern American

If you're a low-key sophisticate with a discerning palate, an appreciation for subtle detail, and sense of adventure, then chef Neal Fraser is your type of

guy, and they speak your language at his superb contemporary American offering in Hollywood. Living up to its name and then some, this earthy lounge and restaurant draws a pretty power crowd, who love to drink, chat, and dine like adults. Fraser marries worldly influences into fine American dishes such as beef carpaccio with green papaya salad, braised pork shank with garlic *rapini* and chorizo home fries, and grilled tenderloin of wild boar accompanied by roastes Brussels sprouts and Yukon gold potato *spaetzle*. Sunday is the outrageously good 'burger night,' while the spectacular dough-nuts of pastry chef Elizabeth Belkind take center stage on Wednesdays (think glazed buttermilk brown butter, bourbon caramel, and malted milk chocolate flavors).

Food 8, Service 8, Atmosphere 8

The Ivy, 113 N. Robertson Blvd (Beverly), Beverly Hills
Tel: 310 274 8303
Open: daily, 11.30am (11am Sat, 10.30am Sun)–11pm (10pm Sun) $70
American

We'd be remiss if we didn't direct you toward this paparazzi-encased power dining institution, where mere mortals have a much better than average chance to dine near celebrities of the A- B- and C-list variety. Behind the darling white picket fence lies the ultrachic French patio where a million big movie deals have been politely signed and sealed. Its inner sanctum

manages to be charming instead of obnoxious, with its country chintzy cuteness. Thankfully, its not all-scene, no-substance... Married co-owners Richard Irving and Lynn von Kersting see to it that their stars are properly satiated. They aren't reinventing the wheel with this menu, and they don't need to... It's all about creature comforts – great big salads, fried chicken, meatloaf, Cajun prime rib, and Irving's exquisite desserts. Much has been made of his chocolate chip cookies.

Food 7, Service 7, Atmosphere 8

Jar, 8255 Beverly Blvd (Harper), Miracle Mile
Tel: 323 655 6566 www.thejar.com
Open: daily, 5.30–11pm $70
American

We love, love, love cozying up with our most clever friends on the brown banquettes of this dreamy, 70s-inspired chophouse, where charming chef Suzanne Tracht puts her spin on pork shank, pot roast, Kansas City steak, and pork chops. Pretty much anything that passes your lips during your meal will knock your fishnets off, from the strong, reverential cocktails to the locally made mozzarella dishes that inspire the menu each Monday night. Tracht's a la carte side dishes are the stuff of legend (particularly the fries), and she's all about scavenging for the freshest flavors of the moment, so you never know what could be amping up the offerings. For a fresh start to your Sunday (if you can get out of bed before 2 p.m.), weasel your way into the brunch, which will pep up your palate, no matter how much booze you downed the night before.

Food 9, Service 8, Atmosphere 9

Mélisse, 1104 Wilshire Blvd (11th St), Santa Monica
Tel: 310 395 0881   www.melisse.com
Open: 6pm (5.45pm Sat)–9.30pm (10pm Fri/Sat). Closed Mon/Sun. $88
Californian/French

If you had been able to play with your food the way chef-owner Josiah Citrin

does his, your parents would have encouraged you to do so all through dinner, every night. Citrin is an affable and capable captain, marrying French flair with Californian approachability, and his obsession with fresh market produce and proteins pays off nightly. Having grown up along these very shores and studied in Paris, he opened this sensational spot in 1999 with his wife, Diane, and earned international acclaim for his bold, ever-changing cuisine. We've swooned over everything from Maine lobster salad with heirloom tomatoes to divine duck breast in

77

cherry sauce with glazed radish and wilted spinach, to the much-adored roasted Jidori chicken with chanterelle mushrooms and broccoli rabe. Citrin is an artist with herbs, and a scientist with flavor combos… Basically, he cooks with confidence, and why shouldn't he? He's a local boy done good.

Food 9, Service 7, Atmosphere 8

Nobu Los Angeles, 903 N La Cienega Blvd (Willoughby), West Hollywood
Tel: 310 657 5711 www.noburestaurants.com
Open: daily, 5.45–11.15pm (midnight Fri/Sat) $80
Japanese fusion

No man has brought more acclaim to the artistry of Japanese cuisine than

Nobu Matsuhisa, and his continuing commitment to high standards, elegant preparations, and uncompromising style continue to earn him a devoted, Black Card-carrying fan base. Indeed, movie stars, supermodels, tycoons, politicos, and sushi snobs alike have the Nobu reservation line on speed dial… so make yours well in advance, if possible. Located in the former L'Orangerie space, his third LA location is decadently decked out – crimson banquettes, sexy low lighting – and is manned by attentive servers and drop-dead gorgeous hosts (naturally). Of course, the *sashimi* and rolls will send you over the moon. If you choose to forego sushi, go for the famous black cod *miso*, Tasmanian ocean trout with *yuzu* soy and crispy spinach, the *Kobe* skirt steak with special Nobu sauces, or the $25-per-ounce Wagyu beef. Isn't it nice to know you'll be properly taken care of?

Food 8, Service 8, Atmosphere 9

Ortolan, 8338 W 3rd Street (Flores), West Hollywood,
Tel: 323 653 3300 www.ortolanrestaurant.com
Open: 6–10pm Tues–Sat $75
French

This is LA, people, and in order to last on this food scene you have to
appeal to the residents' desire for magical transportation, the exacting –
almost unreasonable – standards, the expectation that you will outdo yourself time and time again. Chef Christopher Eme, who wowed the town at

L'Orangerie, is more than up
to the challenge, and his far-out
French establishment crescen-
dos from *amuse bouche*,
through exquisite savory
courses, to dreamy dessert
pastries and conclusive night-
caps. Eme owns and runs
Ortolan with beautiful actress
Jeri Ryan, who can be found
greeting and seating guests
herself. The pair have done up
the space in ritzy, romantic
fashion, meaning sparkling
chandeliers, sweeping velvet
curtains, and a luxurious,
cream-hued palate. Still, it
avoids being stuffy, and therein
lies the magic. Petrossian blinis,
pan-roasted sweetbreads, roast duck leg confit, and crispy pork belly…
Need we say more? Catch a cocktail in the luxe lounge, with its potted
herbs and crackling fireplace.

Food 9, Service 9, Atmosphere 9

Osteria Mozza, 6602 Melrose Ave (Highland), Hollywood
Tel: 323 297 0100 www.mozza-la.com
Open: daily, 5.30pm–midnight $74
Italian

Mario Batali and Nancy Silverton have dug in their heels here on Melrose, and locals have embraced the efforts of these celebrity chefs with open arms. Located next to its equally popular, more casual sister spot, Pizzeria Mozza, the Osteria's fare and extensive Italian wine program have struck a deep chord here. Therefore the reservations take a while to score. (You know what to do... Book early, early, early.) Imposing racks of *vino* are evidence of the team's obsessive oenophile tendencies. Meanwhile, the grand marble 'mozzarella bar' is Silverton's territory, where the finest varieties of the cheese (for which the spot was named) are manipulated in various clever ways. Bulletpoints aside, this is a flat-out fabulous experience, and much deserving of the accolades it has received. Pastas are perfection, like the *gnocchi* with wild boar *ragù* and the decadent ricotta-stuffed ravioli topped with a fried quail egg and drizzled in sage-scented butter. Beyond that, the *porcini*-rubbed rib eye steak pan-roasted sea trout, and grilled quail wrapped in *pancetta* are all worth the hefty bill that awaits.

Food 9, Service 8, Atmosphere 9

Providence, 5955 Melrose Ave (Cole), Hollywood
Tel: 323 460 4170   www.providencela.com
Open: 6–10pm Mon–Thurs; noon–2.30pm, 6–10pm Fri; 5.30–10pm Sat;
5.30–9pm Sun $80
Seafood

The unexaggerated, unspoiled seafood at this critic fave is among the best we've ever had... Executive chef Michael Cimarusti boasts a top tier resume on both coasts, and gained acclaim aplenty by breathing new life into the

Water Grill. Here, he and co-owner Donato Poto keep the intentions pure, the preparations elegant and clean, the décor downplayed yet deluxe, and the servers incredibly well prepared to answer any question you can fire their way. Give into the lobster risotto, foie gras ravioli, or creamy clam chowder (or, as they say, 'chowda') before the real show begins…
Cimarusti's take on wild Alaskan halibut, Tai snapper, and yellow fin tuna are cool looking and he draws out the natural flavors like a snake charmer. Cap that meal off with a milk chocolate and whiskey *panna cotta* and you've done right by your palate.

Food 9, Service 8, Atmosphere 8

Sona, 401 N. La Cienega Blvd (Oakwood), West Hollywood
Tel: 310 659 7708 www.sonarestaurant.com
Open: 6pm (5.30pm Sat)–10.30pm (11.30pm Fri/Sat) Tues–Sat $80
French

David Myers is this great guy… handsome, with shaggy hair and an agree-able attitude and just good vibes coming off him. So maybe it's good karma that guides his success; maybe he's hiding something. But we'll tell you one thing: Sona is a spectacular experience from start to finish. Taking its cues from each season's bounty, the menu is what we might call 'French-plus'… classical techniques, graceful flavor pairings, local ingredients, and artful pre-sentations that make you feel guilty for digging in. Go ahead, but take your time… Food like this was meant to be savored. Some recent homeruns: organic heirloom tomato salad (so pretty!), salt-crusted Elysian Field lamb, and wild sea bass with Ras El Hanout Swiss chard. Leave room for the

81

sweet creations of David's other half, Michelle Myers, at meal's end... Glee-inducing chocolate *beignet*, peanut butter *gelee*, or poached fig tart.

Food 9, Service 9, Atmosphere 9

Spago, 176 N Canon Drive (Wilshire), Beverly Hills
Tel: 310 385 0880   wwwwolfgangpuck.com
Open: 11.30am (noon Sat)–2.15pm, 5.30–9pm (10.30pm Fri/Sat). Closed
Sunday lunch. $77
Californian

Hollywood's elite has flocked to this LA legend since day one – and it's not because the place is 'hot' or 'trendy,' per se... It's because it was built on stylish, sturdy legs. The jewel-toned space is stimulating and sumptuous, the year-round patio is bucolic, the servers know their stuff, and chef Wolfgang

Puck's a wizard. As fine an example of true California cuisine as you're going to find, Spago epitomizes Puck's rich, influential career. The seasonal dishes streaming from the bustling, exposed kitchen (seen through vibrant etched glass) employ the highest quality local produce and meat, and are boundary-pushing without being too 'high concept.' Fare ranges includes haute pizzas, *kabobs*, *quesadillas*, Chinese duck with plum sauce, fire-roasted beef tender-loin, and even some damn good schnitzel. Keep your eyes peeled… Puck likes to talk up the tables.

Food 9, Service 8, Atmosphere 9

STK, 755 N La Cienega Blvd (Waring), West Hollywood
Tel: 310 659 3535   www.stkla.com
Open: daily, 5.30pm–1am (2am Fri/Sat) $80
Steak

While there is no shortage of power steakhouses here in the City of Angels, this sleek, bi-level, ultramodern variation is the top choice of many a power player. Why? It has – and deserves – super-trendy status for fab fare,

a ravishing staff, and sultry décor. Yes, the interior screams, "Let's sign a three-picture deal," with its DJ-manned atrium area and high-ceilinged, banquette-lined dining room. But don't let that fool you… the New York strip and whopping cowboy rib-eye arrive beautifully cooked to order, while the spice-rubbed big eye tuna, roasted lamb porterhouse, and beef short ribs are all first-rate. When you've ceased chowing, let the sexiness continue with its adjoining sister lounge, Coco De Ville. Don't expect to leave without dropping some serious loot. If the experience floats your boat, recreate it the next time you're in New York... the original STK sits on Little West 12th Street, plus a third will spring up in Miami soon.

Food 9, Service 8, Atmosphere 8

Sushi Nozawa, 11288 Ventura Blvd (Eureka), Studio City
Tel: 818 508 7017 www.sushinozawa.com
Open: noon–2pm, 5.30–10pm Mon–Fri $40
Japanese/Sushi

Raw fish rarely comes off as ravishingly as it does at this exceedingly popular spot, overseen by the 'sushi Nazi,' chef Nozawa, a stern-faced raw fish technician who doesn't suffer fools gladly. The sign behind the sushi bar shouts: 'TRUST ME' and trust him, we will. Come knowing there will likely be a sizable line for seats, be patient, and know that when it's your turn you'll be glad you took the time. In business since the mid-90s, Sushi Nozawa has been frequented by  big shots galore who crave melt-away *toro* and ultra-fresh salmon. It goes without saying, but the marvelous creations that make their way to your mouth are lovely to look upon... Too bad they won't be around for long.

Food 9, Service 7, Atmosphere 7

Via Veneto, 3009 Main Street (Pier), Santa Monica
Tel: 310 399 1843   www.viaveneto.us
Open: daily, 6–10.30pm $60
Italian

If you're looking to fan the fires of love or get seduced by a kitchen with all the smoothest moves, make this Italian stallion your next stop. From the

second you step through the door, the venue wins you over with its abundant candlelight, high ceilings, stone floor, and jovial staff. Once seated, it's a steamy culinary rendez-vous… The far-reaching wine list is impressive, and the menu of seasonally inspired classics is hard to choose from. Antipasti take lovely twists and turns, perfectly prepared pastas are embellished with a light hand, and the fresh fish offerings pack big flavors. There are numerous nightly specials, too, so don't rush to make a decision. In fact, don't rush for any reason. (Do make a reservation, though, because these are close quarters, and the local fans will gladly take your place.) Oh, if you're into this sort of thing, one of the three pleasant owners is Warren Cuccurullo of Duran Duran. Rock on.

Food 8, Service 8, Atmosphere 9

Reservations

Notes & Updates

drink...

"Alcohol may be man's worst enemy, but the Bible says love your enemy."
—Frank Sinatra

Ol' Blue Eyes knew how to spread the affection — his favorite paramour being Jack Daniels — and LA's never had a shortage of love nests for an assignation with your poison of preference.

Be they luxurious lounges, down-and-dirty dives, hipster hotspots, old school saloons, classic Hollywood haunts, or eateries where the cocktail scene out-does the menu, what we're talking about here are bars, straight-up — we'll sample the wild and wooly club scene in our Party section, but here we're firmly focused on prime places for avid, enthusiastic, even accomplished barflies to get their drink on.

We've zeroed in on a diverse selection of the most dependably fun-filled, atti-tude-light establishments to knock back a few with a specific kind of local crowd — beach-y, high-class, lowbrow, sexy, scenic, rip-roaring, laid-back, hookup-driven, historic, and just plain cool.

There's a watering hole suited for just about any kind of experience you're looking for. So many, in fact, we have to apologize to the multitude of other great bars we weren't able to squeeze onto the list — if none of our selections are quite right for you, we're sure your LA-based friends have no shortage of suggestions.

Things to know about the bar scene here: for those visitors used to cities where partying until sunup is de rigueur, LA is decidedly not a city that never sleeps. Closing time means 2am if not earlier — we can only theorize the reason

why this is the local standard, presumably because so many in the entertainment industry that rules the town have to be on set for those 5am call times, or maybe just because so many health — and beauty-conscious Angelenos will do anything, even cut their cocktailing short, to avoid having bags under their eyes. Whatever the reason, if you're set on an all-nighter expect to have to bring the party back to your place.

Pub-crawlers should also factor in the daunting sprawl of the city, its ever-snarled traffic and the fact that cabs are never easy to come by. We've kept the list centered on what we think of as the essential LA (sorry, Pasadena, Burbank, and beach city bars), and two of our favorite selections are still 23 miles apart. An extended tour of tippling spots can be time-consuming at best and DUI-dangerous at worst, depending on how many empty glasses you've left in your wake. Plan your transportation accordingly.

So what are you waiting for? We've pre-qualified a ton of great quaff joints — dive in and get to boozin'. Or, as the sign on the pushcart full of hooch Sinatra and the Rat Pack used to wheel onstage said, "Don't think — DRINK."

The Abbey, 692 N. Robertson Blvd (Santa Monica Blvd), West Hollywood

Tel: 310 289 8410 www.abbeyfoodandbar.com
Open: daily, 8am–2am

Perfect to either start the day or end the night, West Hollywood's epicenter of the gay cocktailing circuit has a little something for just about everyone,

with its labyrinthine layout leading from the well-stocked bars to the house music heavy dance floor to the magnificent outdoor Arabian patio to the cozy recessed cabanas (no reservation – a combined $100 tab allows your group to commandeer them). A plethora of pretty boys looking for love gather here, plus lots of their sexy straight-girl BFFs and some non-gay guys working those odds. Who doesn't totally love The Abbey? Only those who dislike hunting for parking, pricey drinks, a jam-packed bar scene, and the fact that the über-hunky bartending staff doesn't swing that way.

Air Conditioned, 2819 Pico Blvd (28th), Santa Monica

Tel: 310 829 3700 www.airconditionedlounge.com
Open: 6pm (7pm Sat/Sun)–2am. Closed Mondays.

A cool, chilled experience, indeed: in the nightlife-starved Westside, this wine, champagne and beer lounge – yes, with cocktails, too – has become a primo gathering place for Hollywood-hating Santa Monicans looking to congregate over Syrah, despite its off-kilter (i.e. kinda grungy) neighborhood. True wine purists occasionally turn up their cork-sniffing noses at some of the selections (available by the bottle or the glass), but the laid back

ambiance, wildly eclectic DJ tunes, the sleek-chic orange-and-mahogany design, and plethora of cheeses make up for any perceived deficiencies in the wine list. Unpretentious is the buzzword here. Sangria lovers unite: Wednesdays offer a 'bottomless glass' for $15.

Bar Lubitsch, 7702 Santa Monica Blvd (N Spaulding), West Hollywood
Tel: 323 654 1234
Open: 6pm–2am Sun–Thu, 7pm–2am Fri–Sat

Film director Ernst Lubitsch's sophistication, wit, and style inspired the term "The Lubitsch Touch" – this namesake bar delivers on all counts, eschewing his Germanic roots for a funkily decadent Russian theme with an emphasis

on riotous red décor and lots and lots of vodkas – 200 types to give your cocktail a kick worthy of the Bolshoi Ballet (the Cucumber Mojito is a house favorite, and the Strawberry

Ninotchka is named for Lubitsch's most famous film with Greta Garbo).
Three distinct sections – the smoking patio, the bustling front barroom and
bangin' back room dance parlor – are always wall-to-wall with wastrels partying like they're in a Bolshevik speakeasy. Just be prepared for Iron Curtain-
long lines and overly KGB-ish security if you arrive after 11pm and consider
slipping the doorman some roubles to ease your entry.

Bar Marmont, 8171 W Sunset Blvd (Selma), West Hollywood
Tel: 323 650 0575   www.chateaumarmont.com
Open: daily, 6pm–2am

At the east edge of the Strip, dodge the club kids for a less drama-filled

sampling of Sunset's party
scene. Don't be confused,
the bar is not inside the
famed hotel, but next door.
Though not the ultra-
trendy hotspot it used to
be, it's still sometimes a
chore to pass the scrutiny
of the bouncer at the distressed fence (reservations
help), once inside you'll
find an opulent, vaguely sin-
ister space (the monarch
butterflies and other
insects stuck to the ceiling
under the glow of red
lanterns suggest a sadistic
hobbyist at work) and a
prime stargazing spot: the
proximity to the privacy-minded Chateau lures A-plus-list stars for cozy
cocktailing, and the menu by chef Carolynn Spense is first-rate. Just come
with cash – parking, among other things, doesn't come cheap here.

Bar Noir at Maison 140, 140 S Lasky Dr (Durant), Beverly Hills
Tel: 310 281 4000 www.maison140beverlyhills.com
Open: daily, 5.30pm–1.30am

It's as if Maison 140, the chic boutique hotel away from prying eyes, deliber-

ately created the perfect martini lounge to carry on an under-the-radar romance… hmmm, wonder if they're in the bedroom-booking business? With a crimson-and-black décor that can only be described as Gallic Zen, the design scheme of the oh-so-cozy space mixes the inn's French provincial feel with an Asian influence that gives it a *wasabi* kick. The end result is an intimate hideaway for sharing an out-of-sight aperitif with your amour.

Boardner's, 1652 N Cherokee Ave (Hollywood), Hollywood
Tel: 323 462 9621 www.boardners.com
Open: daily, 4pm–2am

Oh, the effects of a Hollywood facelift. We loved the bar – a Mecca for Tinseltown tipplers since 1927, in its current incarnation since 1942 – when it was a scruffy, slightly seedy hole-in-the-wall with a storied past (Robert Mitchum drank here, as did W.C. Fields, Raymond Chandler, Ed Wood and even the Black Dahlia herself). But when Hollywood Boulevard finally started hosing off decades of accumulated grime, so too did Boardner's, making itself over as a more luxurious lounge for hipsters and habitués alike, while remaining a no-muss, no fuss watering hole for chatting up friendly strangers and soaking up both its legends and its liquors. Adding a welcome shot of weirdness: the

adjoining Club B-52 is ground zero for LA's underground goth scene.

Cabo Cantina on Sunset, 8301 W Sunset Blvd (Sweetzer), Los Angeles

Tel: 323 822 7820

Open: daily, 4pm (noon Sat/Sun)–midnight

Spring Break is happening on the Strip every day, without the expense of a ticket to Mexico. If you're craving a party-hard frathouse haven filled to overflowing with hotties, look no further than this shakin' shack on Sunset where it feels like it's always happy hour (there's also an after-workier outpost on the Westside, and a beachier berth in Venice). The margaritas are cheap, the Mexican food is edible, the décor is basically a Corona distributor's dream – and yeah, the service is slow but the 'wow factor' of the

otherwise sweet, crop-topped waitresses more than mitigates it. As far as places to go to a) drink; b) work your pickup mojo; and c) failing that, drink some more, Cabo's your ticket to paradise.

Cameo Bar at The Viceroy, 1819 Ocean Ave (Vicente), Santa Monica
Tel: 310 260 7500 www.viceroysantamonica.com
Open: daily, 11am–1am

Genuinely chic cocktail spots near the ocean are in short supply, but the Viceroy's Kelly Wearstler-designed Cameo Bar – so christened for the over-sized white broach that dominates the reception area – is 'opulent' with a capital 'Oh!' Serving as a beachside bar scene for the Westside's cool-but-professional crowd, the shagadellic 60s-influenced English lounge is retro-glam with its parrot greens and pop art purples. The sexy scene spills outside to the pool area and its exclusive, indulgent cabanas, which can be reserved for groups of 10 at a reasonable rate.

Cat & Fiddle, 6530 W Sunset Blvd (Schrader), Hollywood
Tel: 323 468 3800 www.thecatandfiddle.com
Open: daily, 11.30am–2am

If the expansive, Old Hollywood-style Spanish-retro courtyard and gurgling center fountain aren't enough of an eyeful, the people-watching at this enduring British pub is beyond the pale. Brought to its current his-

95

toric Hollywood locale (the 'Casablanca Room' was the site of a scene in the Bogie–Bergman classic) in 1985 by the late British Invasion session musician Kim Gardner in desperation for a place to find a good pint, Cat & Fiddle imported all the usual cliched British amenities – Guinness, fish and chips, dart boards, et al – and serves it up to an artsy, industry-heavy crowd of musicians, starlets, and screenwriters looking for a pubby but hip alternative to the usual Sunset Strip frivolity.

Dan Tana's, 9071 Santa Monica Blvd (Doherty), West Hollywood

Tel: 310 275 9444 www.dantanasrestaurant.com
Open: daily, 5pm–1.30am

From the casks of wine hanging from the walls to the red-and-white checkered tablecloths, everything says Italian, but owner and namesake Dan Tana, who founded the joint in 1964, was a Yugoslavian soccer player (Robert Urich's character in the TV series *Vegas* was named after him). As old school as the environs seem – waiters elegantly clad in tuxedos, busboys in classic red jackets – Tana's is one of the most vibrant and raucous cocktailing scenes in town, drawing big-time billionaires, star athletes, hot heiresses, club-hopping scenesters, gold-digging divas, off-duty detectives, and A-list actors (George Clooney's a regular). Basically anyone, it seems, might walk in to order a drink from Michael, the faux-irascible bartender. If you're inside when the doors lock at 1.30am, you're free to stay and smoke until Maitre d' Craig Susser says it's time to go home.

The Dresden Room, 1760 N Vermont Ave (Kingswell), Los Feliz
Tel: 323 665 4294 www.thedresden.com
Open: daily, 11am (4pm Sun)–2am

As befitting a watering hole in edgy, arty Los Feliz favored by a young, heavily hipster crowd, the Dresden is more ironically cool than anything. Its retro trappings, though authentic, are more kitchy than classy, and the musical talents of its central draw, the venerable, married lounge singing duo Marty

 and Elayne (you saw them, and the Dresden, in *Swingers*), have been open for debate throughout their over-25-year stint here (their version of *Muskrat Love*

proves they're in on the joke, BTW). But damned if they can't kick out an entertaining version of just about any pre-1975 easy listening song thrown at them, and the Blood & Sand, the house's signature cocktail, always goes down smoothly.

Father's Office, 1018 Montana Ave (10th St), Santa Monica
Tel: 310 393 2337 www.fathersoffice.com
Open: 5pm (4pm Fri. noon Sat/Sun)–1am (2am Fri/Sat, midnight Sun)

Hard to characterize yet universally adored – about the best description
we've heard is its own: 'gastropub.' It looks like a simple, low-maintenance,
sit-down neighborhood bar (even on chi-chi shopping street Montana

Avenue), but it's not: it's so popular patrons often wait behind a velvet rope
to enter (a new outpost in Culver City – serving select spirits as well –
may ease the crowds). Everyone says they go there for the deservedly tout-
ed gourmet hamburger, served Burger Nazi style, with absolutely no
requested alterations and no ketchup for the fries, but F.O. is really all about
the beer, with an impressive, almost intimidating selection for ale aficionados
to choose from.

Firefly, 11720 Ventura Blvd (Colfax), Studio City
Tel: 818 762 1833 www.fireflystudiocity.com
Open: daily, 6pm–2am

Firefly's low profile exterior – there's no sign outside, just look for the ivy-
covered wall – adds literal proof to the fact that it's hard to find a hotspot
in the Valley, but the interior shows you don't have to drive over the hills to
find a hip, classy hangout. It's all drawing room chic: draw up to the stately
bar for a cocktail, or sink into the lounge's long couches alongside floor-to-
ceiling bookshelves packed with random volumes to page through, or be
seated around the massive fireplace on the outdoor patio for dinner with

your drinks (reservations, or great patience, necessary) and be tolerant of smokers in the close open-air environs. Fair warning for the bashful: the restrooms are unisex.

Formosa Cafe, 7156 Santa Monica Blvd (Formosa), West Hollywood

Tel: 323 850 9050   www.formosacafe.com
Open: daily, 4pm (6pm Sat/Sun)–2am

Drink in more than just the cocktails; the historic ambiance of this enduring Hollywood hangout is nearly as heady. Established in 1939, the Chinese-themed, red-and-ebony décor appears untouched by time – you half expect to find Ava Gardner whisking in from the studio soundstages next door. In the 1940s gangster Bugsy Siegel made book in the back room (a converted trolley car); in the 1960s Marilyn Monroe and Clark Gable clinked glasses

while making *The Misfits* (the last film for each); in the 1990s Kim Basinger and Kevin Spacey were offered their *L.A. Confidential* roles here (the Formosa cameoed); today stars, both of-the-moment and in-the-making, enjoy intimate libations, but rarely the food, which we can't recommend, at the dim, moody lounge. There's a back room bar for small parties and a rooftop deck for bigger gatherings, and a museum-like collection of head-shots on the wall, hand-delivered by celebs who dallied there over the decades.

Golden Gopher, 417 W Eighth St (Hill), Downtown

Tel: 213 614 8001   www.goldengopherbar.com
Open: daily, 5pm (8pm Sat–Mon)–2am

A favorite among the new haunts popping up in steadily revitalizing Downtown, the Gopher is a revamped speakeasy redone in faux-glam 1970s

stylings – soak in those glitzy chandeliers – and the bearer of one of the oldest liquor licenses in LA (from 1905, which also means you can buy booze to go). You'll find one of the city's most eclectic collections of scen-esters basking in the glow of the gopher-shaped lamps at the dive bar-gone-deluxe. From business types to college kids to the artsy loft crowd, it seems like just about everyone digs the Gopher.

The Griffin, 3000 Los Feliz Blvd (Perlita), Los Feliz

Tel: 323 644 0444
Open: daily, 8pm–2am

Gotta love the cheerfully heavy-handed bartenders in this stiff-drink-standout in a neighbourhood known for its active nightlife scene. The Griffin brings a bit of Black Forest chic to Atwater Village in a cavernous space made remarkable with its dramatic domed brick ceiling, long walnut bars, red leather couches arcing around cozy fireplaces and all the Germanic medieval trappings – and oh, yes, nicotine fiends, that rarest of rare things, an indoor smoking patio. The scene, usually just on the comfortable side of crowded, is young, vibrant and only casually on the make, so you can hook up or drink up at your leisure.

Jones, 7205 Santa Monica Blvd (Formosa), West Hollywood
Tel: 323 850 1727
Open: daily, 2pm (7pm Sat/Sun)–2am

The 144 bottles of Jack Daniels behind chicken wire above the bar confirm this definitely a place dedicated to drink. Always a popular social scene,

Jones' 'it' factor ebbs and flows regularly as newbies discover it causing lines to sometimes crop up, but it's rarely list-y, except for the private room featuring a mammoth Varga Girl-inspired painting. Order dinner if you want one of the booths; the crazy-cozy half-size of some of them can help you get to know a date really well right off the bat. The restroom walls are covered in endless snapshots of Jones-goers flashing intimate areas of their anatomy – we've yet to see such risqué activity actually happening there, but we're excited about the promise.

Liquid Kitty, 11780 W Pico Blvd (Barrington), West Los Angeles

Tel: 310 473 3707 www.liquidkitty.com
Open: 6pm–2am Mon–Fri, 8pm–2am Sat–Sun

The neon sign flashing a cocktail and a cigarette is the come-on, the club's double entendre name (think synonyms – get it?) says the rest. This unassuming martini bar is where the Westside's Pretty Young Things mix, mingle,

and mack on each other amid jazz, Latin, and bluesy grooves. You may need feline vision to navigate in the pitch-black, close-quarter environs, but you just might bump into an attractive new scratching post. If the thrills sound cheap, so are the drinks, which come in glasses big enough to house a goldfish – martinis rule the menu, but there's also a selection of single-malt scotches and the potent Nine Lives Mai Tai. And for musical meowing, Mondays are reserved for Kitty-oke.

Mastro's, 246 N Canon Dr (Dayton Way), Beverly Hills

Tel: 310 888 8782 www.mastrossteakhouse.com

Open: daily, 5pm–11 (midnight Fri/Sat)

Although the principal allure of this elite, upscale steakhouse is its unrivaled menu, the second floor piano bar also consistently delivers the liveliest lounge scene in all of 90210, where monied carnivores congregate to swill

stiff drinks and pour fine wine. Classy, clubby, and a posh playground for sugar daddies, chic cougars, and gorgeous gold-diggers of each gender, it's the sort of swank saloon that evokes Sinatra's swinging heyday. And try, just try to stump impresario Gary Sherer at the piano – and the trumpet, and clarinet, and any other instrument he might decide to whip out – with your request: he has a 5,000-song repertoire.

Marix Tex–Mex Cafe, 1108 N Flores St (Santa Monica), West Hollywood

Tel: 323 656 8800 www.marixtexmex.com

Open: daily, 11.30 am (11am Sat/Sun)–11pm

OK, let's be honest: the wait can be long, the service is so-so, the food is hit-and-miss, and heaven forbid Jennifer Aniston needs a table the night you're there. So why would you want to stop by the quaint little house on Flores that's been converted into a restaurant? Because if you're looking for a place that's raining men – gaggles of gorgeous, gregarious, well-groomed gay men downing pitcher after pitcher of blood-orange margaritas – Marix is a downright down-pour. Skip the *tacos* and come solely for the tequila-soaked singles scene.

Moonshadows Blue Lounge, 20356 Pacific Coast Hwy (Big Rock), Malibu
Tel: 424 644 6450 www.moonshadowsmalibu.com
Open: daily, 11am–midnight (1.30am Fri/Sat)

There's no place better for taking in a magnificent oceanside view of the Pacific with the surf-sand-and-samoleans scene of Malibu while sanguinely sipping your cocktail of choice. Though PCH can be tricky to downright

treacherous (regulars call crossing the highway 'human Frogger') it's well worth it for a visit to Moonshadows' Blue Lounge, where the crashing waves complement the spinning of a rotating crew of DJs delivering house, soul, jazz, world beats, and other mellow mood music. To maximize the romantic, blissed-out vibe, curl up with an intimate on one of the deckside beds, don't let the sometimes slow service raise your heart rate, and keep the Mel Gibson jokes to a minimum.

NoBar, 10622 Magnolia Blvd (Willowcrest), North Hollywood

Tel: 818 753 0545 www.vintagebargroup.com
Open: daily, 7pm (6pm Fri, 8pm Sat/Sun)–2am

One part dive bar and one part haute hipster hangout, NoBar is a bastion for discriminating barflys in the nightlife-challenged Valley. The youthful

crowd is drawn to the combination of its attitude-free ambiance, luxe living room environs (soak up the brown, gold and red felt walls and stained glass bar backdrop), a pool table that takes $1 bills, and the always inventive juke-box selection. A great place to get to know the friendly stranger sitting next to you, and maybe even take a whirl around the unexpected stripper pole, a lingering vestige of a previous incarnation.

The Otheroom, 1201 Abbot Kinney Blvd (San Juan), Venice

Tel: 310 396 6230 www.theotheroom.com
Open: daily, 5pm–2am

Everything you would expect from a watering hole in unconventional Venice, The Otheroom caters to an eclectic scene of young professionals, arty types, and beach bums with a staggering collection of imported and artisan beers and tasteful wines. The wide, open-air window seating is prime for

people-watching along Abbott Kinney, while the spacious bar also abounds with more intimate nooks and crannies. Everything's egalitarian: the staff happily provide take-out menus from local eateries for ordering in food – or bring your own – and your furry best friends are usually welcome guests. Just don't be offended if, on a busy night, the bouncers let locals with Venice driver licenses skip the line to get in – they take care of their own here.

Penthouse at the Huntley Hotel, 1111 Second St (California), Santa Monica

Tel: 310 393 8080
Open: daily, 6.30am–1am

Nestled high on the 18th floor of a classy boutique hotel, the Penthouse's panoramic views of the Pacific are nothing less than stunning, before and after sun-down. The view inside is exceptional as well: casually upscale and drawing a slightly more mature crowd served by an attentive, model-hot waitstaff, the sleek, stark white décor and rich dark wood floors give the impression of cocktailing atop a cloud. Whether enjoying a dinner reservation or just tippling at the bar, the sky-high scene is heavenly indeed.

The Polo Lounge at the Beverly Hills Hotel, 9641 Sunset Blvd (Beverly), Beverly Hills
Tel: 310 276 2251
Open: daily, 7am–2am

Ever rarefied and refined, it's been the ultimate icon of Old Hollywood

glamour, elegance, and privilege since its debut at the 'Pink Palace' in 1937 – the name came four years later as it was the favourite post-polo party spot for a West Coast Algonquin crew including Spencer Tracy, Will Rogers, and Daryl Zanuck. The lavish lounge is past its heyday as the power-dining spot (alas, the famed banquette-side telephones vanished when cellular technology eliminated their necessity for instant deal-making) but still draws an über-mover-and-shaker crowd of industry giants, corporate titans, sports legends, music idols, vacationing royals, and the occasional high-class escort. And if the scene gets a little too old school for your tastes, trot across the lobby to the newer 1912 bar, which skews to a younger breed of power player.

Saints & Sinners, 10899 Venice Blvd (Kelton), Culver City
Tel: 310 842 8066
Open: daily, 5pm–2am

Whether you're feeling devilish (try the Hell Fire – flaming cinnamon liquor and Bacardi 151) or angelic (order the vodka-infused Holy Water), Saints & Sinners has a shot for you. A seemingly nondescript, no-frills hole-in-the-wall on the outside, inside is a 1970s porn producer's dream alcove of questionably opulent taste: oyster shell chandeliers, baroque cupid statuary, gold-flecked bar, a circular fireplace, and velvety wallpaper with orgiastic imagery – and when it's as packed as it often gets you might just feel as if you're in the middle of a group grope. If the tattooed bar staff wasn't already hot enough, just wait until they show off their fire-breathing skills. Naughty, naughty, naughty – and that's nice.

Snake Pit, 7529 Melrose Ave (Sierra Bonita), Hollywood
Tel: 323 653 2011
Open: daily, 11.30am–2am

There's 'dive bar chic' and then there's just 'dive bar,' and the Pit is unapologetically in the latter category (it offers Pabst Blue Ribbon on tap, for goodness sake). Its regular clientele, ranging from Melrose hipsters to sports bar staples to slumming stars and studio execs, often ups the lowbrow appeal (or brings it down, on occasion). The veteran bar staff is one of most gregarious in town, unless, of course, you're annoying them, in which case you'll know about it: the beloved T will boot your butt out herself if you cross her. It's often crowded, about the only frills offered are the tabletop Galaga

game at one of the booths and the seemingly out-of-place Internet jukebox, and it boasts some of the gnarliest bathrooms in town – and yet we loved Snake Pit at first bite, fabulous flaws and all.

Tom Bergin's Tavern, 840 S Fairfax Ave (8th St), Hancock Park

Tel: 323 936 7151 www.tombergins.com
Open: daily, 11.30am–2am

Every great city deserves a truly great Irish pub, and LA received one when Bergin's opened in 1936 – so quintessential that the quaint Irish cottage's

horseshoe-shaped bar served as the inspiration for the *Cheers* set. The food isn't great, which seems somehow appropriate, but the scene certainly is: barflies from 21 to 71 gather to guzzle ale and Irish coffees as fast as longtime bartenders like Michael – one of the city's most memorable characters – can serve them up. You won't receive one on your first or even your 15th visit, but come by enough times and you may be rewarded with a paper shamrock bearing your name, joining the thousands that line the high walls and ceiling (the sharp-eyed will spot early customer Cary Grant's). So yeah, if you're a regular, they always know your name, and they're always glad you came.

Tower Bar at Sunset Tower Hotel, 8358 W Sunset Blvd (Kings), West Hollywood
Tel: 323 848 6677
Open: 6–10pm Mon–Fri, 6–11pm Sat

An oasis of elegance amid the rowdy, crowded Sunset Strip scene, Tower Bar is a high-class alternative for discriminating barflies who want to sample the street's star treatment without all the attendant bullshit that accompa-

nies a Strip outing. As engineered by Maitre d' par excellence, Dimitri Dimitrov, the lounge is all about ambiance and attentive service in refined, relaxed evirons, whether enjoying aperitifs inside or enjoying one of the intimate alcove booths by the pool – believe us, the view of the twinkling LA cityscape is every bit as awesome as the one you get at Skybar, without any of the attitude.

The Well, 6255 W Sunset Blvd (Argyle), Hollywood
Tel: 323 467 9355 www.vintagebargroup.com
Open: daily, 5pm–2am

Truly the 'sweet spot' for all tastes on the Hollywood cocktail circuit, somehow The Well mixes the welcoming, laid-back attitude of a neighborhood

hole-in-the-wall with the chic vibe of an elite lounge, yet there's rarely a line and never a list, and first-timers are treated as warmly as the many regulars. It's sultry, sophisticated, and designed for chilling, yet patrons feel free to get a little wild whenever the oh-so-excellent jukebox blares a booty-freeing tune. The cozy back alcove through wide keyhole passages is perfect, and free to reserve, for private gatherings without being cut off from the rest of the action. The Well runs deep indeed, so drink up.

Telephone numbers

Los Angeles

Telephone numbers

Los Angeles

snack...

When you're taking on a town as lush, lavish, raucous, and strange as Los Angeles, you can't afford to bop around malnourished. And with so many sumptuous, sensational snack spots, there is no excuse for fainting, dehydration, grumbling stomachs, or swooning (unless, of course, you come face to face with a Clooney, McConaughey, or Pitt). Now, we know ... You might be saying to yourself, "It's all fast-food joints around here ... How do I weed out the good from the greasy?" We've assembled a short list of worthy haunts that satisfy every time.

Now, don't be surprised if you're in line to buy coffee and someone famous — say . . . . Courteney Cox, or Lionel Richie — is in line behind you. Understandably, this will be very exciting. Do not turn around and touch the celebrity ... you wouldn't like that if someone did it to you, either. Don't announce the celeb's presence to the room. ("Oh my gosh, it's Fabio!") This is Tinseltown, and stars roam among mortals all the time. At the same time, don't feel like you need to give up your space in deference, or pay for their scone. You have just as much right to be there as they do ... and they can afford their own damn pastry. If you do happen to start a conversation with Courteney, don't bring up your favorite scene from *Friends*. Instead, compliment her blouse, or make an easily returned comment like, "I love this weather!" Still, it's much cooler if you just leave the person be, and say to yourself with satisfaction, "Yeah, Courteney Cox and I have the same taste in baked goods."

OK, back to snacking. This section is separate from our Eat section because of the type of environments you'll be entering, the casual nature of the fare, and the circumstances under which you'll patronize them. We have several Mom-and-Pop greasy spoons that focus on fresh ingredients and comfort food recipes. There is some lovely Mexican fare that must be tried, lest you be exiled from Southern California forever. There is rib-sticking, roll up your sleeves sloppy food and pretty, polite polished food. The diners are all revered by locals so the people watching is always great. And then there are the institutions such as Tommy's for chili burgers and Pink's for hot dogs. Not only are the flavors fab, you know you're in LA every second of the way.

Still, we can't cover every worthy establishment. Fred 62 in Silver Lake is a 24-hour hipster haven where the food is fierce and the waitresses are foxy. Village Pizzeria on Larchmont is one of the best traditional slices you'll find in town, thanks to the owners' Brooklyn pedigree. The Griddle Cafe on Sunset is too tempting for words when your hung-over belly requires sustenance. And here in LA, the coffee chain of choice is The Coffee Bean & Tea Leaf ... You will find outposts all throughout town, though the one on Sunset and Argyle draws an eye-popping crowd of sweatpants-clad actors, directors, gossip columnists, and entertainment industry heavyweights.

All that said, it's time for you to put on a stylish yet totally unassuming ensemble and do your best to blend in with the hungry crowds at one of these memorable snack shacks.

Apple Pan, 10801 W Pico Blvd (Glendon), Rancho Park

Tel: 310 475 3585

Open: 11am–midnight (1am Fri/Sat). Closed Mondays.

You'll feel like you stepped into a bygone era at this highly praised, homey hamburger joint, which has been serving a concise menu of burgers, sand-

wiches, and three kinds of pie since 1947. (Some of the staffers have been working there for nearly as long.) Patrons line up against the walls and wait for a coveted seat at the count-er. It's an unusual ritual for today's fast-food fiend, but obeyed by customers secure in the knowledge that once they sit down they will enjoy a distinctive burger, served sans plate, made according to time-honored tradition and delivering super satisfying taste.

Auntie Em's Kitchen, 4616 Eagle Rock Blvd (Corliss), Glendale

Tel: 323 255 0800   www.auntieemskitchen.com

Open: daily, 8am–7pm (4pm Sat/Sun)

Country charm abounds at this sweet and hearty comfort food joint, where fresh, rib-sticking fare delights an eclectic crowd. They cook seasonally here so the menu continually changes, but what stays the same is a sense of quality and genial atmosphere. Be it the open-faced breakfast sandwiches (roasted asparagus and brie; Cajun turkey sausage), honey orange French toast, the mile-high meatloaf sandwich, the tricked-out tossed Cobb salad, or the veggie-centric offerings that appeal so much to the modern alt-indie hipster

health nut, something is bound to knock your Birkenstocks off. If you've got a sweet tooth, then this is your joint… They love to try out new desserts for willing guinea pigs.

Canter's Deli, 419 N. Fairfax Ave (Oakwood), Hollywood

Tel: 323 651 2030 www.cantersdeli.com

Open: daily, 24 hours

This iconic Jewish deli is a delightfully unrefined holdover from a bygone era, and – much like a *matzo* ball floating in broth – feels plopped down, dense and undeniable, on Fairfax. Everyone from Muhammad Ali to Marilyn Monroe has eaten here, though these days the 24-hour spot has become a favorite hangout of hungry hipsters hunting a late night snack or some hang time in the adjoining lounge, the Kibitz Room. Get a load of these stats: Canter's has pur-veyed over 2 million pounds of *lox*, 9 million pounds of corned beef, 20 million bagels, 10 million *matzo* balls, and 24 million bowls of chicken soup... The numbers don't lie, people. Get thee to this greasy spoon.

In-N-Out Burger, 7009 Sunset Blvd (Orange), Hollywood
www.in-n-out.com
Open: daily, 10.30am–1am (1.30am Fri/Sat)

Founded in Baldwin Park in 1948, this fast-food chain is still family owned and operated, and it has perhaps the most rabid, devoted following of any such chain we know of. The results of this TLC are some of the best burgers in town. With a menu that is almost literally meat and potatoes, the reg-

ulars know that you can always hot rod your Double-Double (two patties, two slices of cheese) in a myriad of ways, from adding more patties to a bun-free version wrapped in lettuce. Our favorite take on an In-N-Out is 'Animal style,' meaning extra pickles, extra spread, and grilled onions. One warning: the fries are made from real potatoes, which means they can be a little limp, so we order ours well done.

King Taco, 4504 E 3rd St (Ford), E Los Angeles
Tel: 323 264 4067 www.kingtaco.com
Open: daily, 24 hours

The original is a cramped spot on Cypress Blvd in Glassell Park, but the jewel in the King's crown is the number two location, which is a 24-hour tribute to the glory of the best tacos in Los Angeles. Mayor Anthony Villaragosa brought Senator Hillary Clinton here during her campaign for

president, which gives some sense of the place's credentials. This location is notable in particular for its inside mural, which is not as good as the food, and for the *taco* trucks that sit in the parking lot to serve the overflow who come for some of the best *carne asada*, *carnitas*, and *al pastor* tacos you can find. It's not all perfect – please skip the gooey nachos – but it's mostly sublime. Not bad for an operation that started in the mid-70s out of a converted ice cream truck.

Millie's Restaurant & Bakery, 3524 W Sunset Blvd (Golden Gate), Silver Lake
Tel: 323 664 0404
Open: daily, 7.30am–3am (4am Fri/Sat)

Rockers chicks and tattooed, sensitive boys need food, too. This diner has been feeding the rocking Silver Lake crowd for some time now, and even used to employ a local notable, Bob Forrest of Thelonious Monster, to boot. These days, the service is quite good, and the food is terrific. They sure know how to make a *blintz* sing, their soups are bottomless, their entrees are comforting even to just think about (pot roast, chicken pot pie, meat-loaf), and desserts are darn good – think everything from tapioca pudding to chocolate cream pie to all-out banana splits. For a bit of hair of the dog happiness, be decadent with chocolate chip French toast or strawberry banana pancakes as you inspect the parade of rumpled folks in slim jeans passing you by.

The Oinkster, 2005 Colorado Blvd (Shearin), Eagle Rock
Tel: 323 255 6465 www.theoinkster.com
Open: daily, 11am–11pm (midnight Fri/Sat, 10pm Sun)

This is one of those brilliant ideas that make you wonder why no one ever thought to do it before: fast food made with fresh, quality ingredients and home-made condiments. OK, maybe somebody did think of this already, but these guys do it right, with terrifically tasty burgers, super-fresh salads, and fries that hold their own against any in LA. It dubs itself 'slow fast food,' and frankly we never mind waiting, as the results are spot on, every time. Bonus: the staff is friendly and upbeat – one of many stark contrasts between this and your average fast-food stop. As the name suggests, the barbecue pulled pork sandwich is something special, but don't count out the rotisserie chicken or classic burgers.

The Original Pantry Café, 877 S Figueroa St (James M Wood), Downtown

Tel: 213 972 9279 www.pantrycafe.com

Open: daily, 24 hours

In business since 1924, this quaint, time-honored institution is currently owned by former Mayor Richard Riordan, and never closes... which is good,

because should you find yourself wanting a generous helping of hamhocks and beans at 3am this would be the place to come. The menu is big – as are the portions – and rich in a range of hearty, home-y dishes. Sirloin tips, short ribs, spaghetti and meatballs, country-fried steak, navy bean soup... these are just a tiny sampling of the grub on offer, and each are prepared with honest-to-goodness lovin' care. Breakfast is a gut-busting affair, so come prepared to adjust a notch in your belt. Do stop in throughout the week for the night-specific desserts. (Our favorite is the Monday night peach cobbler... Divine.)

Philippe the Original, 1001 N Alameda St (Ord), Downtown

Tel: 213 628 3781 www.philippes.com

Open: daily, 6am–10pm

Talk about an authentic LA experience... This place has been in business for 100 years – yes, LA existed 100 years ago – serving up outrageously appetizing, hard-to-rival French-dipped sandwiches, which they claim to have invented by inadvertently dropping one into some roast drippings. Perfect for a pre-Dodgers game bite, the old-time feel of the place comes through in its salads, coleslaw, potato salad, soups, and, oh yes, stewed prunes. They also claim to serve 300 pounds of pigs feet a week, so make of that what

you will. It's a landmark without too much pretension, tons of history, plenty of personality, great food, and good prices… Need we say more?

Pink's, 709 N La Brea Ave (Melrose), Inglewood
Tel: 323 931 4223 www.pinkshollywood.com
Open: daily, 9.30am–2am (3am Fri/Sat)

Known as the undisputed 'hot dog to the stars' – to which its voluminous photo collection of celebrity frankfurter fans will attest – this LA institution

is known for its long dogs and longer lines. Founded in 1939 by Paul Pink, this exalted stand is always entertaining to drive by, as it is one of the most entertaining people-watching spots in town. Be it for the idiosyncratic menu choices (bacon-wrapped dogs or others named after Martha Stewart and Lord of the Rings) or for the way the renowned chili dog lingers with you long after you've headed home, a trip to Pink's is always memorable. In fact, we dare say it is a requirement for any proper visit to the Southland.

Porto's Bakery, 315 N Brand Blvd (California), Glendale
Tel: 818 956 5996 www.portosbakery.com
Open: 6.30am–7pm Mon–Sat; 7am–4pm Sun

This family-run Cuban bakery (and what a charming family it is!) can get ridiculously crowded, so don't go when you're hungry or you could keel over

as you wait to sample the many marvelous items on offer. Ornate cakes (mousses tortes, and traditional), croissants (chocolate, strawberry-cheese, spinach and feta), chocolate chip cookies, macaroons, French baguettes, traditional Cuban treats, and such take center stage, of course, but regulars know that you can score some delicious meat pies, potato croquettes, and Cuban sandwiches, too. Just one look at the divine desserts on display in the glass-front case and you'll be glad you made the trip. Calorie-counters best beware.

Reel Inn, 18661 Pacific Coast Highway (Topanga Canyon), Malibu
Tel: 310 456 8221
Open: daily, 11am–9pm (9.30pm Fri–Sun)

An unpretentious stand (for Los Angeles, anyway) that sits just off Pacific

Coast Highway, the Reel Inn is the place to go when you've spent a long day on the beach, you've got salty hair and sandy shorts, you're starving and in a great mood and want to taste the ocean just a little while longer. Yes, it's a stand, but don't of think this some second rate, overrated spot that's just capitalizing on an

exquisite location... This place serves up generous all varieties of auspicious aquatic delights, from freshly caught tuna to generous fried fare platters. Order from the window, find a spot on one of the picnic benches, and contemplate the vast blue expanse in front of you . . . Or the PCH traffic. There's plenty of that, too.

Roscoe's House of Chicken and Waffles, 1514 N Gower St (W Sunset), Hollywood

Tel: 323 466 7453 www.roscoeschickenandwaffles.com
Open: 8.30am–midnight Sun–Thurs, 8am–4am Fri/Sat

This probably sounds like a weird recommendation if you aren't from around here... fried chicken served with waffles isn't your usual fare. But Roscoe's – all of its various restaurants around town – are veritable institutions, and will take your palate to heavenly places it didn't realize it wanted to go. This is soul food... spicy, messy, fattening, straightforward, and utterly comforting. The menu has plenty more to choose from than the aforementioned fowl and fluffy breakfast fare – think heart-stopping breakfasts, mac and cheese, candied yams, smothered potatoes, greens – but don't stop in unless you're going to take advantage of the house specialty. Sweet potato pie for dessert is never a bad idea, is it?

Señor Fish, 4803 Eagle Rock Blvd (Norwalk), Eagle Rock

Tel: 323 257 7167 www.senor-fish.com
Open: daily, 11am (8am Sat)–9pm

Mostly known for the fish tacos – which are by all means fantastic – this
highly appealing institution scores big with pretty much every item on the
menu. The fish is always going to be fresh, not sketchy, and the sides couldn't

be more authentic if you hitched a ride down south of the border and
scouted some out in a seaside town. Order a grilled piece of halibut and
you'll get a huge piece of delicious fish, rice, beans and a salad for around
ten bucks. Need a *carne asada* burrito? Theirs is killer. Even the fries are
good. But the fish tacos, whether grilled or fried, are things of delicate beauty. Go. Now.

Swingers, 8020 Beverly Blvd (Laurel), West Hollywood

Tel: 323 653 5858 www.swingersdiner.com

Open: daily, 6.30am–4am

A place with this much ironic attitude really shouldn't be as good as this, but that is the marvelous appeal of Swingers. Using pop culture heroes as its theme (highly appropriate in LA, we'd say) and a wide range of comfort and diner food as its mission, this place is dy-no-mite... as resident icon

 Jimmy Walker would say. Feast on this: pork chops and eggs or oat bran pancakes with fruit for breakfast, turkey chili or a jerk chicken Caesar salad for lunch, and steak and fries or right-on turkey meatloaf for dinner. You can build your own healthy smoothie, too, but come on, you only live once: go for a Creamcicle shake or root beer float.

Tito's Tacos, 11222 Washington Place (Sepulveda), Culver City

Tel: 310 391 5780 www.titostacos.com

Open: daily, 9am–11.30pm

You're in LA... it's time to get down with some serious authentic Mexican street fare that you'll remember for years to come. Westsiders swear by Tito's, which boasts huge lines for its cheap, delicious tacos, bean and cheese burritos, and enchiladas. Critics and hungry students have long agreed, and as a result it's always a scene as you wait for your order. In business since 1959, the staff at Tito's has perfected the art of customer service, providing customers with exactly what they want, and it has paid off, big time. Many

call it the best Mexican food in LA – a big claim, but a few bites into the unbelievable beef and bean burrito, stuffed with slow-cooked chili con carne and refried beans, and you'll be quick to agree.

Tommy's, 2575 W Beverly Blvd (Rampart), Echo Park

Tel: 213 389 9060   www.originaltommys.com
Open: daily, 24 hours

Founded in 1946 by ambitious patty purveyor Tommy Koulax, this is the venerable home of the city's most famous chili-topped burger, still operating at its original location at Beverly and Rampart. Amazingly, this jumping joint

manages to serve 15,000 customers a week – and countless more when the place offers its food at the original prices, causing lines to flow up the block – and features numerous

other locations throughout LA, San Bernadino, and Orange Counties. Made to order, an Original Tommy's Burger goes like this, from the top down: bun, pickle, beefsteak tomato slice, freshly chopped onions, Tommy's famous chili, the beef patty, a double-thick slice of cheese, and the bottom bun. Heavenly, every step of the way. Despite the bite that comes from this meaty chili, you'll see patrons at its locations from morning until late at night, which says something about its undeniable popularity.

Urth Caffé, 8565 Melrose Ave (Westmount), West Hollywood

Tel: 310 659 0628 www.urthcaffe.com
Open: daily, 6.30am–11.30pm

By far the hippest purveyors of organic coffees and teas in town (you can often see an Olsen twin downing a concoction in the corner), this munchie mainstay delivers on bohemian charm here in West Hollywood as well as in Beverly Hills and Santa Monica. Alongside the vertically integrated caffeine

creations and rigorously selected tea leaves is an eye-popping array of gourmet pastries and marvelous breakfast/lunch offerings. So, whether you're in the market for some Joe on the go or a big, delicious spread that will keep you glued to your comfy seat for an hour or two, you're pretty much guaranteed to enjoy it. Not so fun is how crowded it gets – and perhaps the clientele can come off a little affected – but such is the price of fame.

Zankou Chicken, 5065 W Sunset Blvd (Mariposa), Los Feliz

Tel: 323 665 7842 www.zankouchicken.com

Open: daily, 11am–11pm

The *Los Angeles Times* has called this the best chicken in the city, joining the legions of diehard fans who have been saying the same thing about this highly agreeable Armenian eatery for years. These birds are magnificent – spit-roasted, tender, flavorful, and featuring a crispy skin so otherworldly we've

actually slapped a wandering hand attempting to sample ours. Go for the hefty half-chicken plates rather than ordering a full order, which doesn't come with the hummus, pickles, or highly addictive garlic sauce. The wraps are also ridiculously good. You can't really go wrong anywhere on the menu – *falafel*, *shawarma*, etc. – and it's cheap, too, making up for its somewhat lackluster location and less-than-lovely décor.

party...

"LA: Come on vacation. Leave on probation." So warns James Ellory, the city's reigning noir-master, and you don't dare doubt him. Even if the *L.A. Confidential* author's literary specialty is the city's epic history of hell-raising hedonism and the holdups, heists, and homicides ingrained therein, today a mere mouse click over to TMZ.com, police blotter to the stars, which daily exposes the makeout sessions, mojito-fueled mishaps and misdemeanors, malfunctioning wardrobes, moving violations, and mug shots that are always around the corner amid LA's deluxe and debauched nightlife scene. So consider the words of the Demon Dog of American Literature carefully.

And then say "Screw it – let's party!" There's just too much enticing naughtiness to be missed.

In LA, trendy scenes can have a lifespan comparable to the average tsetste fly. We assure you that by the time you land one or more of the hotspots we recommend will have a) cooled off; b) closed; c) been replaced with an even more hard-to-crack club; d) drawn an entirely different crowd: or e) all of the above. That said, we've tried to assemble a selection of happening hotspots to suit a variety of moods and tastes – if not exactly evergreen, their shelf lives should be secure for a few seconds more.

Allow us a second to name-check a few more choice options of all stripes for you to Google as a backup: Seven Grand, Winston's, Stone Rose Lounge, Three Clubs, Saddle Ranch Chop House, Lola's, Area, Spaceland, Barney's Beanery, LAX, S Bar, The Avalon, Bigfoot Lodge, 4100, Circle Bar, and the Troubador, to list only a few.

You already know about LA's sprawl and the challenges of club-hopping across the cityscape. Here's another harsh reality: lists and lines are a way of life at some of the most enticing party scenes here – especially because of the high celebrity quotient (or what passes for celebs on the club circuit – keep your cool if the need to admit a Project Runway contestant trumps your front-of-the-line status).

Tips to ease the trauma of the never-ending queue, besides being famous: make advance reservations; go early to beat the door-minders; guys should never travel in packs; work insiders and the Internet to get on promoters' lists; tips and bribes can't hurt, except when they don't work; and for the ladies, showing skin will get you in – some of the time.

As far as adult entertainment options go, despite an abundance of Playmate-perfect bodies and their plastic surgeons, the city hasn't cultivated an especially exciting strip club culture like Las Vegas – due to overzealous ordinances, the options are either fully nude and no booze, or bikini bars and go-go clubs where cocktailing's allowed. Some suggest liberal-minded Angelenos are conflicted over issues of empowerment, exploitation, and artistic expression, but we think it's just that for many of those who might be considering the option there's so much more money doing porn of varying degrees in the Valley – and a hint of fame to boot.

Aside from providing you with the names of a good defense attorney and bail bondsman, we've delivered our end of the deal, so go out and play already... Even if you don't come home with a spotless conscience, at least try to make it back with a clean arrest record.

Coco DeVille, 755 N La Cienega Blvd (Sherwood), West Hollywood

Tel: 310 659 7363 www.cocodeville.com

Open: Tues, Fri & Saturdays until 1.30am

One of the newest and most in-demand hot spots on Hollywood's radar, this 150-person capacity adjunct to the glittering, celebrity-centric steak-

house STK promises a riotous good time if you can squeeze past the ever-present paparazzi and get yourself on the very, very tight list at the door (a promoter hook-up is a near-must, and even then guys will struggle to get in). The décor is fabu-lously funky, with three plush swing seats near the upper-level marble bar and crazy-quilt-colored couches in the bottle-service booths surrounding the kinda improvised, always booty-bangin' dance floor and an enclosed outdoor patio for smokers. Just watch your, ahem, butt in the close confines.

Crown Bar, 7321 Santa Monica Blvd (Fuller), Los Angeles

Tel: 323 882 6774 www.crownbarla.com

Open: daily, 6pm–2am

As the latest 'It' club on the scene, Crown Bar is already claiming its coronet with resplendent regalia: padded walls with textured wallpaper, strategically placed chandeliers, white marble tabletops, studded ottomans, distressed mirrors, and a large, octagon-shaped bar fit for a king – or at least the heavily actor/model/agent/reality star clientele that slips past the tight door. With a lounge, dining area, front patio, and a

dinky dance domain manned by LA's top DJs, the cool-kid club is still being discovered by the A-through-D list and is run by showbiz insiders including a *GQ* editor, so expect its exclusivity to increase by the microsecond.

Les Deux, 1638 N Las Palmas Ave (Hollywood), Hollywood
Tel: 323 462 7644 www.dolcegroup.com/lesdeux
Open: 10pm–2am Tue–Sat

A Hollywood flashpoint for power-partying pretty things thanks to highly publicized patronage by young stars like *The Hills* cast, this hotspot's only cooled by a degree or two. The inevitable door list lends a love-it-or-

hate-it element, but after breeching the velvet rope ever-fashionable club-goers can quaff contentedly in the luxurious Louis XVI environs of the main room, grind to house music in the Ultra Lounge, or simply bask in each other's reflected beauty on the massive patio. Value-added: ringside seats to the frequent catfights that erupt between wasted waifs and overdeveloped D girls – oh, will the scrappers stay in their tiny dresses? – in the parking lot it shares with neighboring rival Element.

The Dime, 442 N Fairfax Ave (Oakwood), Hollywood
Tel: 323 651 4421
Open: daily, 7pm–1.30am

What looks like a dinky dive bar on the outside is actually a surprisingly swank – but still very small – space within, with scarlet walls, smoky mirrors, and babe-alicious bartenders serving up a no-nonsense drink menu. What started out as a luxe neighborhood bar has let a little pretension per-

meate since young celebrity trendoids like Paris Hilton put it on their maps, but if you can slide in early before the velvet rope gets going you'll find that an exceedingly friendly vibe still prevails – thank goodness, since you'll quickly find yourself sandwiched hip-to-hip with the beautiful people.

The Edison, 108 W Second St (Main St), Downtown
Tel: 213 613 0000   www.edisondowntown.com
Open: 5pm–2am Wed–Fri; 6pm–2am Sat

The reinvented site of LA's first power plant in the Higgins Building is visually high voltage, an expansive space characterized by its dramatic architecture

– a mélange of gothic, deco, and industrial, including some of the century-old building's original electrical equipment – and an equally high energy scene varying from thumping promoter nights to live cabaret performances. The hand-crafted drinks are prepared meticulously (the cost reflects the care) and there are even fountains flowing with old school absinthe to complete the steam-punk-meets-speakeasy ambiance. And make sure to dress to impress; the collared-shirt, no-sneakers code is rigidly enforced at the alleyway entrance.

Foxtail, 9077 Santa Monica Blvd (Doheny), West Hollywood,
Tel: 310 859 8369 www.sbe.com/foxtail
Open: 5.30pm–2am. Closed Sundays.

Of the many trendy-to-tragic-in-ten-seconds venues that have been housed in this newly dynamic two-story space, SBE's Euro-style supper club just might be the scene that sticks around. An Art Nouveau pleasure pit of marble, stained glass, embossed leathers, and over-stuffed armchairs, Foxtail's French bistro first floor dining area draws an A-list clientele – reservations are a must and expect the management to exercise elitism, attitude, and celebrity servitude – even as a line forms to gain access to the upper level's exclusive list nightclub loft, which mixes a retro Mod London approach into the decadent mix.

The Green Door, 1429 Ivar Ave (Sunset), Hollywood
Tel: 323 463 0008
Open: 9pm–2am Tues–Fri

A lush and labyrinthine parlour for evoking 1920s Paris that enforces an elite environment for the thirtyish Entourage set (jackets and no sneakers for guys; girls show a little arm and leg). Definitely not a place to just casually roll in – entry is almost always reservation-dependent, dinner or the after-midnight bottle service, which come at premium prices – but even trifles like the truffle mac n' cheese are worth the tab. You're there

for the haute Haunted Mansion ambiance – the courtyard seems straight out of France, and just as smoky – as well as the pleasure of partying with the pretty and the privileged.

Hyde, 8029 W Sunset Blvd (Laurel Canyon), West Hollywood
Tel: 323 656 4933
Open: daily, 9pm–2am

Is there a kinder, gentler Jekyll-esque side to the Hyde experience? Not yet. Known as the epicenter of celebrity bad behavior blurbs in People and Us Weekly, the über-club's cache remains huge, hulking, and haughty

when others so of-the-microsecond shrank to more manageable proportions. Promoter Brent Bolthouse assiduously bars the gate to all but the most insider-y of insiders, so start working on your entry strategy now or you ain't getting in – the tiny spot fits only about 100 people (yes, we've been, and no, we won't describe it, just to keep it frustratingly tantalizing). You know you want in so work it, and work it hard. And if you're turned away in an embarrassing enough fashion, you just might be immortalized in a TMZ video.

Libertine, 8210 Sunset Blvd (Havenhurst), West Hollywood
Tel: 310 270 3122 www.libertineonsunset.com
Open: daily, 6pm–2am

No cover, no list, no line. Reasonably priced, upscale, low-key. And it's off the beaten path yet somehow centered at the heart of the Sunset Strip? Now that's liberating! Libertine is the ultimate anti-club: nestled in a for-

mer apartment building, it effectively has a house party feel, complete with a homey, sofa-friendly living room, kitchen, bedroom-y lounge, stone patio, and a collection of oddball collector's items that makes you feel like if someone doesn't already live there you're ready to sign the lease. Mad-cool music, tremendously tasty menu selections – even the slightly precarious stairwell gives it the kind of character impossible to find (the place ain't easy to locate, either) on the Strip.

Lucky Strike Lanes, 6801 Hollywood Blvd (Highland), Suite 143, Hollywood,
Tel: 323 467 7776 www.bowlluckystrike.com
Open: daily, 11am–2am

Definitely not your grandpa's bowling alley. Far from being filled with league-happy lane-warriors, the neo-nostalgic yet plushly pimped-out Lucky Strike looks more like the *Big Leibowski*'s baked, blessed-out vision of a spare-seek-

er's paradise. It draws a diverse collection of happening hipsters and trendy tourists putting a topspin on the typical nightlife scene, whether renting one of 12 shiny, neon-bathed lanes to bowl a few rounds over beers (reservations recommended, and the plush envrions come at a premium) or chilling at the bar over cocktails, comfort food, and club beats. And some traditions remain the same: you do have to put down a deposit on the bowling shoes – but they're very stylish bowling shoes.

Rage, 8911 Santa Monica Blvd (San Vicente), West Hollywood

Tel: 310 652 2814
Open: daily, noon–2am

No place in WeHo's fierce gay club scene remains as consistent for drawing blessedly young hordes of beautiful boys and lesbian lookers seeking a shiny new toy or two to drink and dance the night away – along with their

straight-chick besties who can shake and shimmy without being grinded on (there is a small straight-guy contingent: some skirt-chasers playing the odds and some metro-sexuals getting their groove on). When the steamy scene gets too hot, literally, the crowd usually spills out onto the street to cool off and converse. Despite its name, Rage isn't a place for haters – it's all about looking for a love connection, if not necessarily a lasting one.

The Rainbow Bar & Grill, 9015 W Sunset Blvd (Hammond), West Hollywood,

Tel: 310-278-4232 rainbowbarandgrill.com
Open: daily, 11am (5pm Sat/Sun)–2 am

In a past life as the Villa Nova, Marilyn Monroe had her first date with Joe DiMaggio here, but at the height of the heavy metal music scene of the 1980s and 1990s, it was where teased-haired titans dined and downed Jack Daniels. From the looks of it today, the rockers have yet to go home (everyone from Slash to Lemmy to Brett Michaels still makes the scene). Practically a Metal Edge museum filled with lazing, leather-vested lotharios

and enhanced hotties hung up on G 'n' R, it's worth a trip for the tattoo-watching alone – and the food in the idiosyncratically Italian bar is roadie-licious. It's as close as you can come to being on tour with Motley Crue circa 1989.

Rooftop Bar at the Standard Downtown, 550 S Flower St (6th St), Downtown

Tel: 213 892 8080 www.standardhotels.com/los-angeles
Open: daily, noon–1.30am

Having matured beyond the B.S. of its trendoid 'In Crowd' origins, the Downtown Standard's rooftop is now for the in-the-know crowd. A cool, attractive collection of locals, students, tourists, and scenesters chill in a classy outdoor lounge (think Art Deco meets Austin Powers) with the most breathtaking view of LA's sky-high cityscape – and a glam poolside scene (not just for gazing at – take a dip if you're feeling frisky) with vibrating space age waterbeds. Bypass the crowded, cover-charged week-ends for a fresher weeknight vibe and feel like you're literally on top of the world.

Skybar, 8440 Sunset Blvd (Olive), West Hollywood
Tel: 323 848 6025 www.mondrianhotel.com
Open: daily, 11am–2am

You're a bit behind the curve if you still think the Skybar at the modernist Mondrian hotel is the ne plus ultra Hollywood hotspot – those days are about a decade past, but it's still a poshly pleasurable, if pricey, place to hang. Instead of going for a glimpse of the glitterati, it offers a glittering view of the LA basin, which works romantic wonders when you're curled up with a companion on one of the cushy poolside beds. Show up early to beat the doorman and take in the sunset, or dine at the neighboring Asia de Cuba and drift on over undisturbed.

Tiki Ti, 4427 Sunset Blvd (Virgil), Silver Lake
Tel: 323 669 9381 www.tiki-ti.com
Open: 4pm–2am Wed–Sat

Launched amid LA's tropical bar craze in 1961, this unpresuming shack keeps the tiki torch burning brightly with nearly 90 distinct exotic drink selections (beer and wine fanciers: wrong bar), including the original founder's famous Ray's Mistake (it's not on the menu, so make yourself sound like a regular). Conversely, only a dozen barstools and a few tables are available, so barflies line up fast and furiously for entrance to a Mai Tai-drenched party scene amid as much kitschy Polynesian paraphernalia as

possible. And because the bar's owner-operated you can smoke like a vol-
cano if it suits you, yet PDAs – even hand-holding – are an ejectable
offense.

Tropicana at the Roosevelt, 7000 Hollywood Blvd (Orange), Hollywood

Tel: 323 769 7260 www.hollywoodroosevelt.com
Open: daily, sunrise to sunset

List-haters take note: though the door minders aren't as notoriously

despotic as at the height of
Tropicana's hipness (even
hotel guests had it tough
breaking through), it's still
best to be connected, arrive
early or get your group to
book a bungalow to lounge
amid the ultimate oh-so-
Hollywood crowd of
wannabes, kind-of-ares,
bigshots, and an Olsen Twin
or two. Designer Dodd
Mitchell marvelously
married Old and New
Hollywood in a chic Mid-
Century Modern oasis of
palm trees, glass, and

chrome under the stars. Revelers often strip down to bikinis or jams (puh-lease, no speedos) for a dip in the city's largest heated swimming pool – with a David Hockney mural underwater – creating a scene both steamy and cool.

Villa, 8623 Melrose Ave (Huntley), West Hollywood
Tel: 310 360 0066
Open: daily, 9pm–2am

So strict about the guest list and dress code it evokes a secret society

(careful pre-planning, owner invitations and return visits beat out passwords or special handshakes), the 150-capacity enclave is as elite and exclusive as they come. Nestled in a two-story site that's housed watering holes since 1919 (everything from silent star speakeasies to neighborhood pubs), Villa's vibe is that of a clubby party inside a Hollywood mansion decorated with eclectic, arty, literary, and downright loopy details (when was the last time you saw a wild animal's furry butt mounted on the wall?). Mondays host 'celebrity karaoke,' where starlets and pop tarts tear through Top 40 tunes.

Backstage Bar & Grill, 10400 Culver Blvd (Motor), Culver City

Tel: 310 839 3892 www.backstageculvercity.com

Open: daily, 11am–2am

An antidote to line-y, list-y, scene-y spots, this unassuming, down-and-dirty dive (dig the 70s ski-chalet chic inside) with its regular folks atmosphere across the street from Sony Studios – Cary Grant was a regular in the MGM era – plays host to one of the wildest no-frills party scenes on the Westside. Karaoke cranks up on Thursdays, Fridays, and Saturdays, and it's blessedly unlikely you'll be shamed out of singing by a bunch of pitch-prefect American Idol-types ready for a music deal – cheers come no matter how badly you mangle Mariah. And the bar food from Misti's Kitchen, deep-frying notwithstanding, is to die for.

Caffé Brass Monkey, 3440 Wilshire Blvd (Mariposa), Koreatown

Tel: 213 381 7047 www.caffebrassmonkey.com

Open: daily, 11am (4pm Sat/Sun)–2 am

While Koreatown is known for its plethora of private-booth karaoke dens, it's awfully fun to show off for more than just your friends. That's where the funky Monkey comes in, tucked out of sight behind a high-rise along the Wilshire Corridor – dark, horribly laid out, and always a bit claustrophobic, crooning in close quarters to pretty new faces is nevertheless an awesome icebreaker. It's short on seating, the wait to warble can seem endless and a few too many professional-sounding singers might steal your thunder, and tipping the KJ doesn't guarantee preferential treatment… But what's a few sour notes among strangers-turned-friends dueting on "Summer Lovin'?".

Harvelle's, 1432 Fourth St (Santa Monica), Santa Monica

Tel: 310 395 1676 www.harvelles.com

Open: daily, 8pm–2am

The Westside's live music standby since 1931, Harvelle's is a blues lover's heaven – a dash of Southside Chicago, a touch of New Orleans' French Quarter, and a pinch of Memphis, all a few blocks from the Santa Monica shore. The cozily narrow club's evolution into a more deluxe den only enhanced its sexy, sweaty scene, and carousing on the checkerboard dance floor feels as delightfully dirty as ever. A minor cover charge provides entry to one of the most rollickin' music rooms in LA with absolutely zero attitude (and Sunday's triumphant Toledo show comes with free waffles!). Just hold your cocktails tight if the cabaret dancers need to commandeer your tabletop for a bit of bump and grind.

Hotel Café, 1623 N. Cahuenga Blvd (Selma), Hollywood
Tel: 323 461 2040 www.hotelcafe.com
Open:

It's almost impossible to imagine that such a drama-free bastion of relaxed live music dedicated to the singer-songwriter exists off an alley in the crazy confines of Hollywood's scene-centric Cahuenga Corridor… but exist it does. The dim, usually acoustic performance room is intimate to the extreme – get there early to snag one of the few tables by the compact stage, or just stand through the set – and for chit-chatting and cigs after there's a tiny piano room off to the side. There's no better place for scouting out the next big thing in the indie-alt-rock world and scarfing brownies at the same time.

Largo at the Coronet, 366 N La Cienega Blvd (Oakwood), West Hollywood
Tel: 310 855 0350 www.largo-la.com
Open: Hours vary nightly; consult schedule online

Relocated from its beloved Fairfax berth to this less intimate but vastly more accommodating digs at the historic, 280-seat Coronet Theater with a huge stage and the smaller 65-seat Little Room, Largo has evolved from eccentric indie darling to a full-fledged but still off-kilter institution. It still regularly hosts experimental performances from musicians like Amiee Mann and Michael Penn and comics like Sarah Silverman and Pattton Oswalt, drawing a wide-ranging audience known for its anti-mainstream tastes. Minus the old distractions of its former food service and whirring bar blenders, the new Largo maintains its cool private-club feel – just with more seats – and remains faithfully all about the show.

The Roxy Theater, 9009 Sunset Blvd (Hammond St), West Hollywood

Tel: 310 278 9457 www.theroxyonsunset.com

Open: daily, 8pm–2am

'Legendary' doesn't begin to do it justice: Neil Young played the 1973 opening and acts from Bruce Springsteen to Miles Davis to Pearl Jam to Amy Winehouse have hit the stage in the intervening years. A bit weathered by the passage of time (we like to believe it was always a little rough around the edges) the Roxy remains the Strip's live music mainstay, as vibrant as it is venerated. The crowded scene is always colorful, whether seated in the booths, gyrating on the dance floor/mosh pit, or bellied up to the bar. And for a more intimate (and less amplified) experience, the On the Rox bar upstairs provides a more mellow escape.

Vibrato Grill Jazz... etc., 2930 Beverly Glen Circle (Beverly Glen), Bel Air

Tel: 424 901 0858 www.vibratogrilljazz.com

Open: 5.30–11pm (midnight Fri/Sat). Closed Mondays.

Established by Tijuana Brass-man Herb Alpert, this romantic, of-a-certain-age scene in richy-rich Bel Air is swank indeed, serving smooth, live jazz straight up alongside sumptuous steaks and seafood. As much care went into the East-meets-West Coast design scheme, with its backlit blonde wood walls, high-backed banquettes, bronze busts of jazz giants like Louis Armstrong, coppery mood lighting, and stucco fireplace, as did into the acoustics, which were crafted by Albert's own sound team. Those seeking an upscale escape from LA's youth-dominated nightlife scene where grownups can gather to groove on relaxing riffs will find no false notes here.

ADULT

4 Play Gentleman's Club, 2238 Cotner Ave (Olympic), West Los Angeles

Tel: 310 575 0660 www.4playclub.com

Open: daily, noon (7pm Sat/Sun)–2 am (3am Thurs, 4am Fri)

The locale for LA's most beautiful dancers, hands down (and hands off,

mostly), in a particularly posh setting (baroque bordello meets Studio 54), 4 Play cuts straight to the chase: the knockouts gloriously gambol fully nude, with extra-late hours and extra-long lap-, couch-, and bed-dances offering plenty of opportunity to study every inch of their taught, toned, personally trained torsos. Low on raunch, high on style, but also sassy and spirited, it's a favorite for both Westside power players and UCLA students alike – the steady stream of curious female customers calmed by the chic surroundings is a bonus. And if it matters, the menu is as tasty as the eye candy.

The Body Shop, 8240 W. Sunset Blvd (Roxbury), West Hollywood
Tel: 323 656 1401 www.thebodyshophollywood.com
Open: daily, noon–5am

If you must sample the strip clubs on the Sunset Strip (which generally run too skeev-o for our refined tastes), the Body Shop's probably your best bet given its cool-cachet neighborhood and hard-rockin' history as either a location or inspiration for every music video set in a neon-soaked adult club you've ever seen (Motley Crue fans note the 'Girls Girls Girls' signage). Its legendary topless 'n' cocktail scene is no more in favor of all-nude naughti-ness, always at least a few drop-dead delicious dancers doing their thing. It's a money pit of inconsistent experience, for sure, but stays true to its nasty roots: in the risqué private rooms anything may go – until she decides it doesn't.

Jumbo's Clown Room, 5153 Hollywood Blvd (Winona), Los Angeles
Tel: 323 666 1187 www.jumbos.com
Open: daily, 4pm–2am

Known as the best place to find a pleasing panoply of poledancers grinding in g-strings to The Smiths or Led Zeppelin – from tattooed barely legals to experienced over-40s, appealingly unaugmented hotties to off-kilter cuties, Suicide Girl sirens to questionable chromosome arrangements, Jumbo's per-fected dive-diva appeal and offered something for everyone (a pre-fame Courtney Love being the most auspicious alum). It still does, only now keep-ing their chi-chis clad in its less lascivious 'bikini bar' incarnation… damn those city ordinances. But you can still quaff cheapie cocktails while eye-balling the acrobatics, and even with their tops tied down the gals are as game as ever.

Plan B, 11637 W Pico Blvd (Barrington), West Los Angeles
Tel: 310 312 3633 www.planb-club.com
Open: daily, 6pm–2am

Going against the oft-cheesy go-go girl grain, Plan B comes off more as a
first option for the discriminating sophisticate looking for a supper club
experience with a fair share of sleek, semi-naked ladies entertaining in an
elegant setting… far more high-falutin' than Hooters, for sure. Offering the
closest thing to gourmet fare for a gentleman's establishment along with
Cristal, fine cognacs, and choice cigars, the Old Boys Club vibe is livened up
by the Young Girls, Playmate-level posers in lingerie and swimwear, and the
liberal-minded lady customers who like the lush location.

Sam's Hofbrau, 1751 E Olympic Blvd (McGarry), Downtown
Tel: 213 623 3989 www.samshofbrau.com
Open: daily, 11am–2am

Don't let the name or the portly Teutonic bartender hoisting a *stein* on the
old school signage fool you… this isn't a German beer garden with the
bonus of bikini babes, though it does specialize in *zaftig*, of the all-natural
variety. It's a no-frills, no-cover, no-drink-minimum, no-pressure juggy joint
servicing a hard-working Downtown crowd (be wary: the 'hood is diction-
ary-def 'seedy') and home to some of the most happy-go-lucky but occasionally hard-assed hardbodies circling the pole (they'll tell you exactly what
you can't get away with). The place, the dancers, and the vibe are so retro-
quirky-cool, is it any wonder semi-regular Quentin Tarantino made it a location in *Jackie Brown*?

Telephone numbers

culture...

"I don't want to live in a city where the only cultural advantage is that you can make a right turn on a red light." – Woody Allen, *Annie Hall*

"I love Los Angeles. I love Hollywood. They're beautiful. Everybody's plastic, but I love plastic. I want to be plastic." – Andy Warhol

Forget what you may have heard about the cultural scene in Los Angeles... Believe it or not, it is vibrant, growing, eclectic, and valid on a global scale. People like to take digs at Lalaland's level of refinement because, hey, for a long time that simply wasn't the focus out here. Nowadays, they're just jealous, because the city's tastemakers have used their wealth and prestige to draw world-class fine art, music, theater, and dance to town. It's all a great fit; the movie and music industries thrive on the shock of the new, and everybody's always looking for people willing to push boundaries. With 4 million residents and 25 million annual visitors drawn to LA's dream factory appeal, it's an ideal place to unveil fresh ideas.

From the local government to the universities to the philanthropic wealthy population, those with the means to transform the ditzy reputation of LA have opened countless doors for artists and performers, and the community has

embraced these efforts with open arms. Sophisticated collectors showcase important works in their glamorous homes all around town, while gallerists from Downtown LA, WeHo, Beverly Hills, and Santa Monica court world-class talent. Meanwhile, the celebrated museums play host to important exhibits and boast spectacular permanent collections. Best of all, local artists are free to let their minds wander, thanks to the placid weather and vibes… and as a result the town is constantly energized by the spirit of creativity.

Beyond that, there are a million great opportunities to be entertained, be it the ballet, improv comedy, film festivals, the LA Philharmonic, or simply the movies. Yes, this is one of those rare cities where it is totally acceptable to take in a blockbuster during your vacation. Why? Because Angelenos live and breath cinema, and they treat their theaters like temples of worship. In fact, once you've enjoyed your two hours of big screen fun and the credits start to roll, you'll notice that nobody gets up. They're all reading the screen to find their friends, or simply praying to the celluloid gods, saying, "Please let them pick up my pilot!" "Please let them cast me in that slasher flick!"

Don't forget, LA is home to the world's greatest musicians, and as a result there are numerous noteworthy concerts every night of the week. Whether you're a jazz aficionado, a metalhead, a Top 40 disciple, or a classical music snob, there is something on the roster for you. On that note (ha), LA features the greatest radio on earth. Take a moment to notice this as you cruise down Santa Monica in your rental with the windows rolled down. Our personal favorite is Indie 103.1, the best alternative music station ever, which plays tons of local bands as well as the greatest un-bubblegum offerings of all time.

So, for these and many other reasons, peruse the following listings and prepare to be impressed.

ACE Institute Of Contemporary Art, The Wilshire Tower, 5514 Wilshire Blvd (Burnside), Hancock Park

Tel: 323 935 4411 www.acegallery.net

Open: 10am–6pm Tues–Sat

This grand space is worth a visit solely for the forgotten pleasure of being ferried from the street level up to the gallery by a genial elevator operator. Once there, you'll find large, airy rooms and halls that have hosted a wide range of shows, from the photography of Dennis Hopper to amazing exhibitions by the likes of Tara Donavan, who use the rooms for maximum, mind-boggling impact.

ACME, 6150 Wilshire Blvd (Fairfax), Hancock Park

Tel: 323 857 5942 www.acmelosangeles.com

Open: 11am–6pm Tues–Sat

Sitting inconspicuously across the street from a discount store, ACME is part of a small, buzzworthy scrum of galleries tucked off Wilshire. This compact space is possibly the best of the bunch, having hosted stellar shows from artists such as Uta Barth, Joyce Lightbody, and Laura Owens. A real treat, ACME. frequently participates in combined openings with the adjacent galleries, creating lively events filled up with groundbreaking art and prime people watching.

The Brewery, 2100 N Main St (Moulton), Lincoln Heights

Tel: 323 342 0717 www.the-brewery.net

Open: noon–5pm Fri–Sun

Located in an industrial area off the I-5, the former Pabst Blue Ribbon and East Side breweries has been turned into a warren of studios, galleries, and living spaces for artists and designers. The combined use of the area gives it the feel of a village, albeit one that incorporates whimsy into the looming red brick buildings.

Chung King Road (N Hill St), Chinatown

Think LA's Chinatown is only notable for its role as the backdrop for Jackie Chan's *Rush Hour*? Think again. The area known as Chung King Road has developed into a solid art scene, a quiet alley lined with stores selling Chinese art mixed with newer galleries such as Sister and Black Dragon Society, which focuses on contemporary work. These galleries are just minutes from MOCA and the Geffen Contemporary, not to mention dozens of places to eat.

The Hammer Museum, 10899 Wilshire Blvd (Westwood Blvd), Westwood

Tel: 310 443 7000 www.hammer.ucla.edu
Open: 11am–7pm (9pm Thurs, 5pm Sun). Closed Mondays.

Founded by the former head of Occidental Petroleum Company and originally devoted to older works, the museum now is run by UCLA and focuses on what it calls 'the art of our time.' Whatever you call it, it's very good. Parking is cheap and easy (a rarity in Westwood) and the bookstore is top notch.

The Huntington Library, 1151 Oxford Rd (Orlando Rd), San Marino,

Tel: 626 405 2100 www.huntington.org
Open: 10.30am (noon winter weekdays)–4.30pm. Closed Tuesdays.

Are these the loveliest grounds in Los Angeles? You'll get no argument from us. The former home of Henry Huntington boasts a variety of different gardens – succulents, roses and a Japanese tea garden – as well as art galleries and one of the most astounding collections of rare books and manuscripts in the world. Check out the Gutenberg Bible, let the kids run wild in the children's garden and stay for high tea. Or a glass of wine.

The J. Paul Getty Museum, 1200 Getty Center Dr (N Sepulveda Blvd), Bel Air

Tel: 310 440 7300 www.getty.edu
Open: daily, 10am–6pm (9pm Fri/Sat)

The Getty site is amazing, a museum complex that sits on a hillside overlooking the city. Take the tram up and stand in awe of the marble and glass structures, manicured lawns and gorgeous gardens and plantings. The exhibitions can be hit or miss, but it's a lovely place to spend an afternoon - just be sure to make a reservation online ahead of time to ensure you will have a parking space.

LACMA (Los Angeles County Museum of Art), 5905 Wilshire Blvd (Spaulding), Hancock Park
Tel: 323 857 6000 www.lacma.org
Open: daily, noon (11am Sat/Sun)–8pm. Closed Wednesdays.

Known for its high-profile exhibitions, impressive permanent collection, and Steve Martin's rollerskating escapade in *LA Story*, this impressive institution has been undergoing a multimillion dollar upgrade and improvement project. For all its strengths (and a few weaknesses) as a museum, LACMA's also a wonderful place just to hang out, whether you come to check out the nearby La Brea Tar Pits or to listen to the free concerts or banjo players, or just want to stop in for a bite at the excellent café.

MOCA (Museum of Contemporary Art), 250 S Grand Ave (S Flower St), Downtown
The Geffen Contemporary at MOCA, 152 N Central Ave (E 1st St), Downtown
Tel: 213 626 6222 www.moca.org
Open: 11am–5pm (8pm Thurs, 6pm Sun). Closed Tues and Weds.

The two museums are relatively close (though a slightly longer walk than most Angelenos would care to take) and focus on recent works as well as the gems from the permanent collection. A single fee gets you into both (as well as the MOCA Pacific Design Center in West Los Angeles), and you can easily visit both in an afternoon. Plus, if you end your trek at the Geffen, you're in Little Tokyo and can decompress with a bowl of *udon* or sweet bean cake.

Santa Monica Museum of Art, Bergamot Center, 2525 Michigan Ave (Cloverfield), Santa Monica
Tel: 310 586 6488 www.bergamotstation.com
Open: 10am–6pm Tues–Fri, 11am–5.30pm Sat

Located on the site of a former trolley stop dating back to 1875, this complex of galleries and architecture and design firms and the Santa Monica Museum of Art is a delightful, walkable space that offers a rich mix of contemporary art. And, with the exception of the museum, it's free. Once you've had your fill of art, there's a fine café to sit and discuss what you've seen.

Attend the Taping of a TV Show Audiences Unlimited, Inc.
Tel: 818 753 3470 www.tvtickets.com or TVTIX 323 653 4105

Watch your favorite shows get made by attending the taping of a TV show. Better yet, get yourself on a game show like *The Price Is Right* or *Wheel of Fortune* and take home some loot from your visit. Some tapings can be tedious, but it's free and how often do you get the chance to do this? Chances are, whether you're at Paramount Studios on Melrose or CBS on Fairfax or elsewhere, there will be a nearby bar or restaurant that knows just what you need.

Downtown
Union Station/Olvera Street/Broadway/Farmers' Market

Though it's been overshadowed by its surroundings over the years, the Downtown area of Los Angeles has much to offer: museums, restaurants, and the main branch of the public library. And a terrific way to explore the area would be to stop in at Union Station, the city's 1939 wonder that has been used in countless movies and videos. Then wander over to Olvera Street, the oldest part of the city and a taste of old Mexico (not to mention touristy LA). From there you could explore Little Tokyo or Chinatown, or perhaps catch a tour of old movie houses that line Broadway or grab a bite at the downtown Farmers' Market.

Griffith Park/Observatory/Universal City Walk

Just what any city dweller needs: nature that you don't have to travel far to get to. Griffith Park boasts the Los Angeles Zoo, the Autry National Center, the Griffith Observatory, a carousel, a golf course as well as acres of grass, trees and places to picnic or ride on one of two mini train tracks. Had enough? Hop on the freeway and you're just a few minutes from the more urban pleasures – shopping, restaurants, concert venues, IMAX theater – of Universal City Walk.

Hollywood and Highland/Chinese Theater

Get your fill of Hollywood lore in one gulp. The Hollywood & Highland Center contains the Kodak Theater, home of the Academy Awards, as well as numerous places to eat and shop. And this area is rich with Tinseltown must-sees like the Walk of Fame, the Chinese Theater, and the must-be-seen to be believed array of celebrity impersonators who line the streets in the guise of everyone from Elmo to Captain Jack Sparrow hoping to raise a little cash off the tourists who photograph them.

Santa Monica Pier/Venice/Third Street

Want to do something unusual in Los Angeles? Take a walk. Santa Monica's Third Street offers all the amenities of a real city thoroughfare, with a few improvements. Watch the street performers, shop in the upscale boutiques and eat, eat, eat. As well, the promenade is within walking distance of the Santa Monica Pier and a short hop to Venice's funkier environs.

BALLET, OPERA & THEATERS

Alex Theatre, 216 North Brand Blvd (Wilson), Glendale
Tel: 818 243 7700 www.alextheatre.org

Built in 1925, this theater has had an eclectic past as a vaudeville theater and a movie house. And it's still eclectic, hosting Miss Asia beauty contests and Armenian language concerts and movie nights. It's got the look of classic theaters, and chances are there's something on its calendar that you might enjoy.

Geffen Playhouse, 10886 Le Conte Ave (Westwood Blvd), Westwood
Tel: 310 208 5454 www.geffenplayhouse.com

A one-time Masonic lodge and furniture store, this magnificently renovated space has been consistently turning out top-quality theater pieces for the past 15 years. Its proximity to Hollywood means that you'll find some of the city's finest performers working here.

The Groundlings Theater, 7307 Melrose Ave (Poinsettia), Hollywood
Tel: 323 934 4747 www.groundlings.com

Want to go to the theater, but don't want to see, you know, theater? Consider spending the evening with the Groundlings, the city's pre-eminent improvisational comedy group. The launching pad for Pee Wee Herman's Paul Reubens, Phil Hartman, Lisa Kudrow, and more, it's a live show that's always lively.

The Hollywood Bowl, 2301 N Highland Ave (Hollywood Bowl Rd), Hollywood
Tel: 323 436 2827 www.hollywoodbowl.com

Not only does it host all the top rock shows, the Bowl is an incredible place to take in a night of symphonic music. Whether you prefer serious classical music or John Williams conducting an evening of movie themes, you'll find what you need here. Pack a picnic and enjoy a relaxing and lovely way to hear live music.

Mark Taper, 135 N. Grand Ave (Temple), Downtown
Tel: 213 628 2772 www.centertheatregroup.org

The home to many of LA's finest productions, the Taper has a well-earned reputation for great theater, including the world premieres of *Children of a Lesser God*, *Angels In America*, and *The Kentucky Cycle*. Currently undergoing a $30 million renovation, the soon-to-be-reopened space promises good things in the future.

The Music Center, 135 N Grand Ave (1st St), Downtown
Tel: 213 972 7211 www.musiccenter.org

This has been the Downtown center of the city's arts for years and for good reason. Whether you're seeing an opera at the Dorothy Chandler or a play at the Ahmanson or just want to sit and watch the fountains spray in the courtyard, this is culture's home in L.A.

Pantages, 6233 Hollywood Blvd (Argyle Ave), Hollywood
Tel: 323 468 1770 www.pantages-theater.com

Formerly the home of the Academy Awards, this grand old theater in the heart of Hollywood still plays host to the big out of town shows that take up residence here, such as the musicals Wicked and The Lion King.

Pasadena Playhouse, 39 S El Molino Ave (E Green St), Pasadena

Tel: 626 356 7529 www.pasadenaplayhouse.org

Founded in 1917 in a old burlesque house, the Playhouse has been the eventual launching pad for actors such as Gene Hackman and Dustin Hoffman, and in recent years has developed a reputation for its commitment to diversity and its entertaining mix of revivals and brand-new works. Additionally, it has a charming courtyard space, perfect for an intermission conversation or snack.

Royce Hall, 340 Royce Drive (Sunset Blvd), UCLA

Tel: 310 825 2101 www.uclalive.org

Having hosted performances by George Gershwin, Duke Ellington, Philip Glass, and many more, this structure – the design of which is based on a 10th-Century Italian church, continues to attract the best of the best of the performing arts, including dance pieces, readings, and concerts featuring musicians from around the world. Located on the UCLA campus and possessing amazing acoustics, Royce is one of the finest performances spaces in the world.

Walt Disney Concert Hall, 111 S Grand Ave (2nd St), Downtown

Tel: 323 850 2000 www.disneyconcerthall.com

You'll see it whether you go inside or not. The undulating silver waves of Frank Gehry's design have refocused downtown on this architectural wonder, the latest addition to the Music Center family. Don't miss out on enjoying a performance because the sound is magnificent. The affiliated Redcat performance space hosts some of the most innovative works in the city.

El Rey, 5515 Wilshire Blvd (Dunsmuir), Hancock Park
Tel: 323 936 6400 www.theelrey.com

Best if you score a table, as this converted dance hall tends to favor the taller members of the audience. Or just stand in the back if you don't mind the sound of the bartenders digging into the ice. Regardless of its few short-comings, it's a lovely venue with good sound and they consistently book top-notch acts.

The Greek, 2700 N Vermont Ave (Commonwealth Canyon) Griffith Park
Tel: 323 665 5857 www.greektheatrela.com

The storied Greek, located in Griffith Park, makes every show an event. There's something about the open-air seating that makes everything more festive. Though larger than the adorable John Anson Ford, the Greek's layout creates intimate settings when even the largest crowds are in attendance. The parking isn't ideal, however.

Hollywood Bowl, 2301 N Highland Ave (Hollywood Bowl Rd), Hollywood
Tel: 323 436 2827 www.hollywoodbowl.com

This is the ultimate place in Los Angeles to see a show in the summertime; whether you're there to see the Philharmonic with fireworks or the long days of the Playboy Jazz Festival or some of the wonderful rock shows they host, such as recent pairings of indie rock bands with string orchestras, you will be enchanted. Even if you're sitting on the concrete seats all the way in the back, you need only feel the cool temperatures (bring a sweater) and look up at the stars and be transported. Traffic and parking can be a hassle, so consider taking a shuttle if you can.

Staples Center, 1111 S. Figueroa Boulevard, Downtown
Tel: 213 742 7340 staplescenter.com

It lacks the storied history and well-seasoned patina of venues like the Hollywood Bowl or the Forum, but this is the city's 800-pound gorilla of music and sports watching. And it's pretty nice: a clean, easily navigated venue smack in the middle of Downtown that's close to all the freeways.

The Wiltern, 3790 Wilshire Boulevard, Los Angeles
Tel: 213 388 1400

It's gone through plenty of alterations and renovations over the years, but this venerable hall has retained what's important: a warmth and atmosphere that makes it a lovely place to see a show, whether you're there for the bluegrass of Nickel Creek or the hammering intensity of Metallica.

MOVIE THEATERS

Arclight, 6360 W Sunset Blvd (Morningside), Hollywood
Tel: 323 464 4226   www.arclightcinemas.com

The site of the legendary Cinerama Dome, which has been upgraded with the new surroundings, the Arclight is a movie lover's complex: lots of films, assigned seating, and clean, well-maintained theaters. You can also get a drink or a dessert in the café. Just don't be late for the show. They won't let you in the theater.

The Bridge Cinema Deluxe, 6081 Center Dr (Sepulveda Blvd), Crenshaw
Tell: 310 568 3375   www.thebridgecinema.com

They call it 'Cinema De Lux,' and basically this is the fancy-schmanciest way to see a film in town outside of your own private screening room. Wall-to-wall screens, leather seats, concierge service, and a lounge, it's, well, fancy. Some might want to save this for dates or special evenings, but you can also enjoy the latest Adam Sandler movie or kiddie flick in this luxurious environment, too.

El Capitan, 6838 Hollywood Blvd (Highland), Hollywood
www.disney.go.com

Located just across the street from Hollywood and Highland complex, El Capitan is an old movie palace that thrived and survived, due in large part to the success of the parent company which took over its operations,

160

Disney. The theater is clean, well appointed, and still in use unlike some of the movie palaces on Broadway downtown. It's also got an organ and that's always cool.

Nuart 11272 Santa Monica Blvd (Sawtelle Blvd), West Los Angeles
Tel: 310 281 8223   www.landmarktheaters.com

The hands-down most beloved art house in the city, the Nuart has the charm of a classic, neon-lit movie house with the sensibility of a sharp cineaste. Just go.

Silent Movie Theatre, 611 N Fairfax Ave (Clinton St), West Hollywood
Tel: 323 655 2520   www.silentmovietheatre.com

Following the shocking murder of its owner in 1997 in the theater's lobby, the theater has been sold, renovated, and turned into a spot for wrap parties and private events. The current owners have been experimenting with all kinds of clever film programming, too. It is definitely worth a visit for something different.

shop...

Whether you're looking to score a rare vintage find, trendsetting fashion, unique jewellery, or gifts to take back home, LA has you covered. After all shopping is one of the city's serious pastimes (after movie making, apparel manufacturing, and looking good). From pleasant malls and luxury boutiques to independent designer shops and quirky home stores, your biggest challenge will be fitting it all in since the city sometimes seems like a never ending sprawl.

They say that nobody walks in LA (which is practically true compared to New York or Paris), but there are several shopping districts that are perfect for parking the car and taking an afternoon stroll. The quiet, tree-lined Melrose Place is all about luxury shopping (Oscar de la Renta, Monique Lhuillier, Marc Jacobs, and more), but without all of the tourists who congregate on Rodeo Drive (right) daily.

West Third Street – just east of the Beverly Center mega mall – is famed for its collection of independent boutiques often stocking edgier fashions than you'd find in the beach towns. For a more urbane feel, try La Brea – smack in the middle of the city – where cult sneaker shops are housed next to upscale designer boutiques.

For celebrity spotting it's all about Robertson Boulevard, where several blocks are packed with trendy boutiques, a new Chanel store, and the famed Ivy restaurant where you'll see the paparazzi camped out. It's worth a trip out to the celeb-heavy Malibu Country Mart where shopping and a stunning view of the Pacific come together.

If you're the kind of person who doesn't hesitate dropping a couple grand on a new outfit, you'll want to tackle Beverly Hills. Between Neiman Marcus, Saks Fifth Avenue, Barneys New York, and every luxury brand from Louis Vuitton to the jaw-dropping Prada Epicenter store, you'll have no problem emptying your wallet on these fancy streets.

Across town, Hollywood Boulevard is full of kitschy souvenir shops and LA staples like American Apparel where you can pick up inexpensive cotton gear made locally. Funkier, creative types will want to hit Los Feliz, a charming village of unique finds (no major designer labels here) and Silver Lake, an artist community where the streets are lined with tattooed guys and gals who beat to their own drum.

If you're more into one-stop shopping just hit one of LA's shopping centers, such as The Grove, an outdoor mall with dancing fountains, Hollywood &

Highland, a massive mall that's also home to the Kodak Theatre (where the Oscars are held), or Fred Segal, a collection of hip stores that is known for starting rather than following the trends.

In this section we bring you the top shops that truly define LA, from the legendary Beverly Hills shops you see in the movies to more under-the-radar boutiques where you can take home a one-of-a-kind find. The icons and the emerging shops are covered so you don't have to play hit or miss. You'll discover everything that's unique about LA shopping: sexy shop girls, surprisingly friendly service, cutting-edge design, and plenty of valet parking. Bring an extra suitcase because nobody comes home empty handed!

Barneys New York *9570 Wilshire Blvd* An emporium of style, Barneys brings together top designers – 3.1 Phillip Lim, Lanvin, Derek Lam, and Manolo Blahnik for example – along with beauty brands, men's, home, and baby, all under one roof

Chanel *400 North Rodeo Dr* Featuring the full Chanel range, specially created Chanel artwork, and a façade inspired by the Chanel No. 5 perfume box that lights up with LED lights at night

Christian Louboutin *9040 Burton Way* The famed footwear designer's signature red soled shoes – some with $895 price tags

Dior *309 North Rodeo Dr* From glitzy gowns worthy of the red carpet to sparkling costume jewelry

Fendi *355 North Rodeo Dr* All things Fendi – including a design-your-own baguette bag computer – are housed at the redesigned boutique

Gucci *347 North Rodeo Dr* Sleek and modern décor is a suitable setting for Gucci's range of collections, from ready-to-wear to home items and accessories

Louis Vuitton *295 North Rodeo Dr* You could spend a day inside Vuitton's mega-sized LA flagship. Sure there are the bags, but head upstairs for understatedly chic ready-to-wear and fine jewelry

Martin Margiela *9970 Santa Monica Blvd* Edgy fashion from the elusive Belgian designer in a jaw-dropping space featuring a tower of champagne glasses and gypsy sequined façade

Miu Miu *317 North Rodeo Dr* A 1,500-square-foot emporium of all things Miu Miu in a French boudoir setting

Neiman Marcus *9700 Wilshire Blvd* Top designers, beauty brands, a well-loved footwear department, and gifts all under one roof

Prada Epicenter *343 North Rodeo Dr* Wildly inventive architect Rem Koolhaas designed Prada's progressive and fantastical multi-level store

Saks Fifth Avenue *9600 Wilshire Blvd* The luxury goods retailer (where Winona Ryder was arrested for shoplifting) offers multiple floors of fashion and a men's store

LA CIENEGA/ROBERTSON/ WEST HOLLYWOOD

Anya Hindmarch *118 South Robertson Blvd* It's all about luxury accessories – handbags, shoes, and small leather goods – at the British designer's jewel box shop

Boule *408 North La Cienega Blvd* Pale blue walls, the most decadent edible confections and insanely chic hat box packaging at David Myers' modern patisserie

Curve *154 North Robertson Blvd* Another 'it' boutique for the super skinny and fashion forward set

Intermix *110 Robertson Blvd* All the latest tops, dresses, accessories, and shoes from designers like M Missoni, Diane von Furstenberg, and Stella McCartney

Kitson *116 North Robertson Blvd* You may notice a throng of flashbulbs out front of celeb-magnet Kitson, where it's all about the latest trends. There's a Kitson Men and Kitson Kids on Robertson as well

Lisa Kline *136 South Robertson Blvd* You can't miss the mud flap girl logo at Lisa Kline, a regular destination for fashion lovers and flashbulb seekers

Opening Ceremony *451 North La Cienega Blvd* An icon in New York, Angelenos were thrilled when the edgy designer shop (known for collaborations with Chloe Sevigny) debuted on the Left Coast

Stella McCartney *8823 Beverly Blvd* The witty Brit brought a bit of England to LA with her romantic two-story salon featuring the entire Stella McCartney range

Sunset Plaza *8623 Sunset Blvd* Sidewalk cafés, European flair, and hot boutiques – from Tracey Ross and D&G Dolce & Gabbana to Catherine Malandrino and Calypso – make Sunset Plaza a favorite for those seeking a shopping stroll. A hot bed of high style, you'll find body-conscious offerings at H Lorenzo Women, well-tailored men's wear at Scott & Co., and plenty of animal prints at Just Cavalli.

Tory Burch *142 South Robertson Blvd* It's all about bold geometric prints, chic caftans, and vivid color at American designer Tory Burch's self-titled boutique

Trashy Lingerie *402 North La Cienega Blvd* You'll need to buy a $5 annual membership to shop Trashy's iconic lingerie shop, where 30 seamstresses and patternmakers are on staff

MELROSE/MELROSE PLACE/MELROSE HEIGHTS

Agent Provocateur *7961 Melrose Avenue* A sultry salon of expensive lingerie, sexed up shoes, and even stylish pasties for those who want to get naughty

Alexander McQueen *8379 Melrose Avenue* A spaceship-like shop with a nine-foot metal sculpture, VIP room, and jaw-dropping fashions for men and women.

Balenciaga *8670 Melrose Avenue* Architectural and futuristic (the boutique and the clothes), at luxury prices.

Decades *8214 Melrose Avenue* Twentieth-century vintage couture and accoutrements for men and women. Visit neighboring DecadesTwo for 21st-century designer resale.

Fred Segal *8100 Melrose Avenue* See-and-be-seen at this unique collection of shops where trends are born and designers are made. The indoor-outdoor shopping center houses a flurry of boutiques, including Ron Herman where you'll find contemporary styles, Fred Segal Feet for the latest footwear, and Apothia for the latest beauty brands. Visit Fred Segal in Santa Monica on 5th Street between Colorado and Broadway.

John Varvatos *8800 Melrose Avenue* Preppy, stylish, rugged and hugely elegant menswear for the post-metrosexual generation

Jonathan Adler *8125 Melrose Avenue* Fans of the fashionable potter come to peruse the largest selection on the West Coast of lighting, bedding, furniture, rugs, tabletop items, and of course, pottery

Marc by Jacobs *8410 Melrose Avenue* More affordable than the Marc Jacobs boutiques across the street, the designer's diffusion boutique offers chic threads, well-priced accessories, and fashion books

Marni *8460 Melrose Place* Eclectic (and high-priced) fashions that women from all over the globe covet

Monique Lhuillier *8485 Melrose Place* Indulge your every wedding gown fantasy and peruse eveningwear in a 4,200-square-foot atelier featuring vast fitting rooms, high ceilings, and towering windows

Oscar de la Renta *8446 Melrose Place* Gorgeous gowns, sexy sandals, and an upstairs home store that mixes modern and island aesthetics

Paul Smith *8221 Melrose Avenue* A 5,000-square-foot pink box filled with striped button downs for guys, dapper loafers, and the only US locale to stock the entire women's line

Sergio Rossi *8424 Melrose Place* Shoe fetishists can't get enough of the Italian luxury brand's footwear and accessory boutique

West 3rd/Beverly/Fairfax/La Brea

American Rag Cie *150 South La Brea Avenue* Unique fashion finds, including women's, men's, denim, shoes, accessories, and vintage

Beverly Center *8500 Beverly Blvd* A hot spot for decades, the Beverly Center – anchored by Bloomingdale's, Macy's, and Macy's Men Store – features 160 specialty boutiques and restaurants. Whether you're looking for designer duds (D&G, Calvin Klein, Gucci), contemporary looks (Kenneth Cole, A|X Armani Exchange, MAX&Co.) or beauty shops (Sephora, M.A.C., Victoria's Secret Beauty), you'll be covered.

Buffalo Exchange *131 North La Brea Avenue* New and recycled ever-changing fashions where customers can bring in former favorites to trade or cash on the spot

Des Kohan *671 Cloverdale Avenue* A destination for an expertly edited selection of Viktor & Rolf, Hussein Chalayan, Helmut Lang, and vintage Chanel and Givenchy

Flight 001 *8235 West 3rd St* Named for the legendary PanAm flight, you'll find all things travel, including stylish luggage, groom bags, and gadgets

Hillary Rush *8222 West 3rd St* A well-edited women's boutique that has plenty of celeb fans, chic jewelry, and exclusive labels

Nanette Lepore *8420 Melrose Avenue* Feminine and flirty frocks are the specialty of the pale pink colored house.

Presse *326 South La Brea Blvd* Two former fashion editors have brought some of the best talent – Doo. Ri, Vena Cava, and Balmain – to their haute shop

The Grove *189 The Grove Dr* An outdoor wonderland known for its dancing fountains, old-fashioned trolley, and proximity to the LA Farmers' Market, The Grove has no shortage of shops. There are the old standbys (Nordstrom, Gap, Banana Republic, Abercrombie & Fitch, Quiksilver Boardriders Club), home furnishings (Crate & Barrel, Pottery Barn Kids) and more fashion forward selections at Barneys New York CO-OP, Theodore, and Michael Kors.

The Way We Wore *334 South La Brea* A Mecca for vintage clothing from fashion encyclopedia Doris Raymond. Designers and celebs can't get enough of the couture, but there are more affordable pieces from the Victorian era to the 1980s.

Traveler's Bookcase *8375 West 3rd St* Every travel book you'll ever need (basically ours and you know it) with super-cool knowledgeable staff who just get it

Trina Turk *8008 West 3rd St* You can't help but smile inside Trina Turk's 1960s-inspired shop featuring orb lighting, rose-colored walls, and her line of fun frocks and bold prints

Zipper *8316 West 3rd St* Form meets function at Zipper, where you can find amazing gifts — books, entertaining, personal accessories — for anyone on your list

Santa Monica/Pacific Palisades/Malibu

Elyse Walker *15320 Antioch St* Three shops on one block featuring high-end accessories from Prada and Marc Jacobs, ready-to-wear from all the major fashion houses and the latest basics by Vince, Splendid, and C&C
Happy LA *542 Palisades Dr* Boutique by the beach decked out with Missoni towels in lieu of dressing room curtains and plenty of denim, easy separates, and dainty dresses
Il Primo Passo *1624 Montana Avenue* A Mecca for shoe fiends in search of a place to worship, Beth Whiffen's eco-friendly shop is stocked with Lacroix, Zanotti, and Pucci
Kiehl's *1516 Montana Avenue* The famed apothecary is beloved by Angelenos who favor the effective products, clean packaging, and oversize samples
London Sole *1331 Montana Avenue* It's all about the ballet flats at this diminutive, English-inspired shoe shop
Malibu Country Mart *3835 Cross Creek Rd* With new stores from Sigerson Morrison, John Varvatos, and 7 For All Mankind and old standbys like James Perse, Ralph Lauren, Juicy Couture, and Shabby Chic, it's no surprise that even the most urbane city dwellers make the drive along PCH to shop at this high-end center that draws Hollywood A-listers in droves
Planet Blue *800 14th St* This LA chain of shops — outposts are in Malibu, Venice, and Beverly Hills — is where you're likely to spy Paris or Lindsey picking up the latest contemporary designers
Sigerson Morrison *23410 Civic Center Way* Chic sandals, sexy pumps, and the label's signature flats at the 1,500-square-foot minimalist shop
Third Street Promenade *Third Street between Wilshire Blvd and Broadway* Pedestrian-friendly outdoor shopping at its finest with shops from Anthropologie, Diesel, Club Monaco, Banana Republic, J. Crew, French Connections, Puma, and many more just blocks from the beach. With a flurry of restaurants, movie theaters, and street performers, it's easy to make an entire afternoon or evening out of the dusk-till-dawn Promenade.

Brentwood/West Los Angeles

Apartment Number 9 *225 26th St* Polished casual looks for the guys from Seize Sur Vingt, Stevan Alan, and Trovata

Black Market *2023 Sawtelle Blvd* Casual, but stylish fashions, plenty of rare sneakers and rotating art on the walls at this hangout for teens, UCLA kids, and grown up skaters

Footcandy *11934 San Vicente Blvd* LA gals have been known to drop ten grand in one visit on Louboutin's, Choo's, and Manolo Blahnik's at the elegant shoe salon

Giant Robot *2015 Sawtelle Blvd* With two quirky shops on Sawtelle (full of toys, comics, and skater stuff) and the restaurant GR/eats, you'd think the guys from Giant Robot magazine were taking over the Westside's Little Tokyo

Intuition *10581 West Pico Blvd* Celebs and Hollywood stylists shop Intuition for all the latest fashion and jewelry trends

Marie Mason Apothecary *225 26th St* A beauty haven filled to the brim with candles, perfumes, skin care, home fragrance, and custom blended scents

Ron Herman *11677 San Vicente Blvd* Known for eye-catching window displays, lots of denim, and lots of designer labels

Los Feliz/Silver Lake/Echo Park

A+R *1716 Silver Lake Blvd* Inventive and modern home décor items sourced from around the globe

Everything's Jake *4644 Hollywood Blvd* Jonathan Kanarek's menswear shop is a place of worship for all things vintage, from old school ascots to rockabilly suits

Show Pony *1543 Echo Park Avenue* Feathers, fur, spangles, and chiffon come together at artist Kime Buzzelli's chic boutique known for one-of-a-kind finds and local designers

The Circle *2395 Glendale Blvd* Indie designer outlet for those willing to sift through the racks

Undefeated *3827 West Sunset Blvd* With other locations on La Brea and in Santa Monica, the sneaker retailer is a must for the latest street style

White Trash Charms *1951 Hillhurst Avenue* LA's cool girls visit WTC regularly for sweet and sexy charm jewelry and fashions from RVCA and Karen Walker

Y-Que Trading Post *1770 North Vermont Avenue* Makers of the famed 'Free Winona' shirt, Y-Que is a first stop shop for all things snarky

Hollywood/Larchmont

American Apparel *6922 Hollywood Blvd* Made in America mostly cotton offerings known for snug fitting, 1970s-era wear, and sexed up ad campaigns. There's another shop a few blocks away, not to mention more than 10 other LA area outposts.

Amoeba *6400 West Sunset Blvd* The best record store in LA draws indie lovers, goth gals, Latino rockers, and jazz fans alike

Hollywood & Highland *6801 Hollywood Blvd* The $615 million mega mall plays home to the Kodak Theater, a flurry of restaurants and Spa Luce at the Renaissance Hotel, but most tourists come for the stores: H&M, Louis Vuitton, BCBG, Gap, Guess, bebe, Lucky Brand Jeans, Virgin Megastore, XXI Forever, Sephora, Oakley, and many more. Adjacent to the famed Mann's Chinese Theatre, Hollywood & Highland is like a movie set in itself, with its imposing archways, grand staircases, and mammoth pillars topped by marble elephants.

Kicks Sole Provider *143 North Larchmont Blvd* Black and white checkered Vans, Converse Chuck Taylor All-Stars, Adidas Superstar shell-toes, and the latest limited edition styles

Sonya Ooten *238 North Larchmont Blvd* Chic gem bar in the heart of quaint Larchmont Village, stocking Ooten's signature precious metal jewelry featuring precious and semi-precious stones

Downtown

Apartment 3 *1855 Industrial St* Vintage and independent designer apparel for guys and gals alike

Blends *125 West 4th St* Hardcore sneakerheads flock to Blends for limited edition releases and some of the boldest kicks from Nike, Puma, and Reebok

Brooks Brothers *604 South Figueroa St* It's all about tradition, tailoring, and total prepsters at Brooks Brothers, an emporium of khaki pants and navy blazers for the whole family

Pussy & Pooch *565 South Main St* A super modern pet haven of all things for your dogs and cats, including stylish beds, spa products, and chic leashes

Shopping List

play...

There is very little you can't do in and around Los Angeles. The temperate weather and inexhaustible imagination of its inhabitants ensures you'll run out of vacation days before you run out of things to do. Want to water ski? You got it. Take a helicopter to a small island? Of course! Ride a Segway, learn to surf and fly on a trapeze? You can fit all that in before sunset.

La-La Land is famous for its many storied attractions, of course: Disneyland, Sea World, Universal Studios Tours. Those are nice daylong excursions. But you didn't come to LA to be surrounded by tourists, did you?

Instead, take in a Lakers basketball game at the Staples Center. (Any non-sports-loving companions will at least enjoy spotting celebrities in the crowd.) LA has two baseball teams (though one is technically in nearby Orange County). And though it may defy logic for a desert town to host an ice hockey team, LA has two of those as well.

If you'd rather play sports than watch them, join a pickup game of basketball or volleyball along the beach in Santa Monica. Or bike along any of the 44 miles of trails that run north from Torrance Beach all the way to Will Rogers State

Beach, just below Malibu. Mountain biking is also exquisite (and in some places excruciating) in the Santa Monica Mountains and inside the wild confines of the Angeles National Forest.

Hikers will enjoy finding the ruins of old mansions, breathtaking ocean vistas and hidden waterfalls (well, more like water-trickles) along the many hiking paths along the coastline.

For less strenuous adventures, LA offers a variety of guided tours to satisfy the most eclectic interests – murals, stars' homes, even grisly crime scenes. If it can be categorized, it can be packaged for your amusement.

Los Angeles is also home to some of the world's best shopping and urban spas, particularly around Beverly Hills. This well-manicured neighborhood requires well-manicured neighbors, so you'll find no shortage of indulgent spas to pamper to just about any predilection. Go during weekday mornings when regular working stiffs are chained to their cubicles, and you just might share a steam room with a celeb.

Of course, LA is most famous for the biggest star of all (in our solar system, anyway): the sun. While rainstorms are not unheard of, Los Angeles does enjoy a preponderance of sunny days. Relax along miles of coastline with just a book, a bathing suit, and nary a care in the world (and if you want to skip the bathing suit part, LA offers a few good beaches for that, too).

Head west, young men (and women) if you're looking to worship the sun in proper LA style. Here, a sampling of the beaches that line the PCH (that's the Pacific Coast Highway to you and me non Lalaland habitues) and kiss the glorious Pacific. Surfers, check the Northern Surf Report at 310 457 9701.

The Beach Cities: Hermosa Beach, Manhattan Beach, and Redondo Beach

This trifecta of famous beach burgs conjure all the dreamy mythos of SoCal culture, with their tourist-friendly municipal piers, combed stretches of beach, world-class surfing, beach volleyball, and exquisite sunsets. These shores have seen many a film crew – everything from *Point Break* to *CSI: Miami* to *The O.C.*, and celebs from Demi Moore to Jack Black to Henry Rollins grew up here. For a good time, clean your glasses and follow the Strand, the famous walk path that snakes from South Redondo north to Santa Monica.

Huntington Beach, 400 Pacific Coast Highway

This stretch of Orange county shoreline, north of Costa Mesa, offers happy surfers a unique 'south swell,' and daytrippers near-perfect weather (save for the gloomy month of June).

Santa Monica Beach

The beachiest of all beaches, this sandy, two-mile Mecca begs that you conjure Gidget and Moondoggie as you scope out its volleyball players, grab a picnic, and stroll its famous pier. At the Pier's end sits the iconic Looff Hippodrome Carousel, surrounding by family activities and snack shacks.

Surfrider Beach, Malibu

This legendary spot off the Malibu Pier boasts a coveted 'right break' and draws world-class wave riders from across LA County.

Venice Beach, Ocean Walk, Venice

One of the most colorful spots in all of Lalaland, Venice Beach is home to

Muscle Beach (where the Governator used to pump iron), the ever-entertaining skate dancing plaza, the zany and colorful promenade, and courts for basketball, handball, and paddle tennis. It's the Xanadu-Baywatch-Grease-style California dream, come alive around you

Zuma Beach, 30000 Pacific Coast Highway, Malibu

Ideal for swimming, surfing, and people watching, this famed beach plays host to several major surf competitions and basically offers everything you want in a SoCal beach – clean water, tanned lifeguards, rich teens, and spectacular views.

CYCLING

Perry's, Santa Monica and Venice Beach
Tel: 310 452 7609 www.perryscafe.com

There is no shortage of bike shops in LA, but precious few would offer to serve you burgers on the sand after taking you on a guided beach bike tour. Perry's has eight locations in and around the pier and offers bikes for a reasonable price. Rentals run about $9/hr or $25 for a full day depending on what kind of bike you want – and they have all kinds: mountain bikes, cruisers, tandems, adult trikes, and even in-line skates. The staff are helpful and will supply you with detailed maps of the city's 44-mile beach bike path. If you're tuckered after the ride, Perry's Beach Butler service will set you up with a towel, table, umbrella, and served lunch on the beach after your ride (about $100 for the day).

HIKING

Inspiration Point Loop (Will Rogers State Historic Park), 1501 Will Rogers Park Road, Pacific Palisades
Tel: 310 454 8212

This none-too-difficult three-mile loop starts and finishes at Will Rogers' home. Overlooking LA from downtown to the ocean, the trail reaches its apex at a flat knoll that's wonderful for picnics. Park docents also offer tours of the former screen star's impressive home.

Runyon Canyon, Franklin and Fuller Avenue, Hollywood
Tel: 323 666 5046 www.laparks.org

This 130-acre park, two blocks from Hollywood Boulevard, shows off some of LA's best vistas: the Hollywood sign and the Griffith Observatory to the east, Downtown to the south, and (on clear days) the Pacific Ocean and Catalina Island to the south west. But try not to get too distracted by the views: this is a favorite spot for LA's beautiful people to run their dogs, so make sure to watch where you step!

Solstice Canyon, Intersection of Pacific Coast Highway and Corral Canyon Road, Malibu

Halfway up the path of this secluded, beautiful trail, you'll find an abandoned 1865 stone cabin. But far more impressive is Tropical Terrace nearby. It was once an extravagant canyon home with a colorful glass walkway, but now it's a mysterious bit of rubble near a calming stream and little waterfall along a lush hiking trail. One of LA's true hidden gems.

The Stairs, Adelaide Drive (4th Street), Santa Monica

Want to know how LA hotties stay so outrageously fit? Step up. And up. And up. Keep stepping. Harder than any gym workout and cheaper than… well, than anything that isn't free, these 189 concrete steps serve as one of LA's hottest (and hardest) workout spots. The whole tree-lined residential area around the stairs feels like an outdoor gym, with people stretching and lifting weights on grassy traffic islands. This being LA, don't come in old sweats – people are here to see, sweat, and be seen sweating. Insider's tip: the wooden stairs a half-block north are easier on the knees.

HORSEBACK RIDING

LA Horseback Riding, 2623 Old Topanga Canyon Road
Tel: 818 591 2032 www.losangeleshorsebackriding.com

Three nights a month, experienced guides take riders on 90-minute excursions under the full moon. The rest of the month, the rides aren't too shabby either: guided rides are offered through the tranquil trails of the Santa Monica Mountains from morning until dusk every day – even most holidays.

NUDE BEACHES

Abalone Cove Shoreline Park, 5970 Palos Verdes Drive South, Rancho Palos Verdes
Tel: 310 377 1222

Abalone Cove is made up of two beaches – Abalone and Sacred Cove. Both are known for their breathtaking tidepools, but only at Sacred Cove can tidepool buffs be in the buff while they clamber about. Warning: wear shoes with good traction for getting down to the beach from the parking lot. Parking: $5 per car.

Black's Beach, La Jolla
www.sandiego.gov/lifeguards/beaches

If you find yourself in San Diego, you should find yourself at Black's Beach. This not-so-secret nude beach is one of the best places to, ahem, let it all hang out. But keep it clean. This is a family-friendly nude beach, and the regulars are pretty good at schooling less-decorous newcomers about the rules. High cliffs and poor walkways make access to Black's Beach difficult. It's best to walk (clothed) along the shore from the north or south, provided the tide gives you passage.

PICK-UP BASKETBALL

Barrington Park Recreation Center, 333 S Barrington Avenue (Sunset), Brentwood
Tel: 310 476 4866

This small, safe park is packed with well-toned, competitive players and offers great pick-up games. Which is why you might have a long wait to play.

PICK-UP VOLLEYBALL

2030 Ocean Avenue (Bay), Santa Monica
Tel: 310 458 2239

Though the city typically offers classes here in the summer, pick-up games can be had all year round. Warning: If you're going to play volleyball in open sunshine with everyone watching you make sure you're good, because your opponents will be.

SAILING

After a few days of maddening traffic, you might want to leave the freeways for the waterways. Charter a yacht for a day – or even a week – and cruise around the coast. Or head out to the open seas and spot whales and dolphins as you sail to the small island of Catalina Island, a lovely vacation spot 26 miles off the coast of LA.

> **Bluewater Sailing, 13505 Bali Way (Lincoln), Marina del Rey**
> Tel: 310 823 5545 www.bluewatersailing.com

Bluewater offers would-be skippers lessons in sailing basics, but landlubbers are advised to rent a boat with a captain for their first times out. Charter prices vary from $50 to $2,695, depending on the type of boat and length of trip.

SEGWAY

> **Segway Los Angeles, 1660 Ocean Avenue (Colorado), Santa Monica**
> Tel: 310 395 1395

The city's only authorized Segway dealership serves Santa Monica, Venice Beach, and Malibu – though Segway enthusiasts are cautioned to stick to the Santa Monica and Malibu paths, as Venice Beach cyclists tend to hog lanes and view Segway riders with scorn. The staff are friendly and lenient when it comes to rental times/rates, but typically rentals are priced at $75 for 2 hours. Guided tours are also available.

SHOOT YOUR OWN PORN FILM

Inspired by all the glitz and glamour of Tinseltown, you and your intended (or maybe even an Internet random or even your very own real life pornstar) may decide to engage in the mother of all DIY projects: making your own 'blue movie.' These are modern times, and there's nothing wrong with unleashing your inner Jenna Jameson. Do, however, keep the following in mind:

Editing and camera skills. Don't expect to yield a tantalizing work of carnal art by propping your camcorder up on top of the TV and getting down to business missionary-style. You've got to be creative, go in for the first-person visuals, mix up the body placement, play up your strong suits. ("Check out the knees on that dude. Hot.") Be conscious of lighting – the old 'scarf over the lampshade' trick still works – and remember to face into the light for clarity, away for illusion.

Be realistic. Unless you've been crunching and squatting and pushing up weight a bunch for the last year, not every angle is going to be flattering. Be aware of gravity when leaning forward, and note that sex has an inherent hilarious quality to it that will likely be caught on camera.

Supplies. Have water and, you know, 'goo' at hand, not to mention proper prophylactics in case this ain't your partner's first time at the rodeo. Also, towels… Sweating profusely all over someone's face or back is not hot.

Implications. Home-made porn may seem like a great idea while utterly drunk, but in the sobering morning light you might become yoked by regret. If your computer becomes compromised or you break up under nasty circumstances, you may discover yourself as a star on Xtube.com. (Or, God forbid, ChubbyAction.com.)

Pick up some naughty apparel at Hustler Hollywood (8920 W Sunset Boulevard, West Hollywood, 310 860 9009), or bondage gear and sexy extras at Rough Trade (3915 W Sunset Boulevard, 323 660 7956).

For camera and tripod rentals, hit up Indie Rentals (1350 N. Highland Avenue, Hollywood, 323 465 7700; indierentals.com).

For a real life porn actress, with DVD releases and porn awards under her belt, try www.pamelapeaks.com – who claims she can bring the likes of Chasey Lain to the party. Rates are high, but in this town everything's negotiable.

Esotouric Bus Adventures Into the Secret Heart of L.A.
Tel: 323 223 2767 www.esotouric.com

Buses team down Rodeo Drive every half hour, but how many venture off to East LA for 'Black Dahlia and Nicotine' flavored gelato? From culinary oddities to famous crime scenes to points of architectural importance, this band of brainy, funny history buffs introduces tourists and natives alike to the hidden ingredients that make up the strange soup that is Los Angeles. Most tours, $58.

Starline Tours
Tel: 800 959 3131 www.starlinetours.com

Of all the bus lines that will take you on tours of the tall gates and security cameras that obscure celebrities' homes, this one is the most famous and well-established. Prices vary but are in the $40 range.

SPAS

Burke Williams, 8000 Sunset Blvd (Laurel Canyon), West Hollywood
Tel: 866 239 6635 www.burkewilliamsspa.com

With multiple locations around Los Angeles and Orange County, Burke Williams could easily suffer from its ubiquity. But this is hardly the McDonald's of spas. Skilled services, attentive staff and luxurious digs feel world-class. The spa offers clients generous use of its saunas, steam rooms, and hot tubs, so even a simple mani-pedi can feel like a full day at the spa.

Dtox Day Spa, 3206 Los Feliz Blvd (Glenfeliz), Griffith Park
Tel: 323 665 3869 www.dtoxdayspa.com
Open: daily, 10am–8pm (6pm Sat/Sun)

This 6,000-square-foot spa boasts waterfalls and a giant Buddha – and, oh yeah, incredible wraps, scrubs, and other treatments to help slough off the pore-clogging effects of too much LA smog.

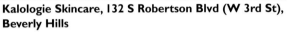

Kalologie Skincare, 132 S Robertson Blvd (W 3rd St), Beverly Hills

Tel: 310 276 9670   www.kalologie.com
Open: daily, 10am–7pm Mon–Sat; 11am–6pm Sun

Offering everything from Botox to eyebrow waxing, the medical staff and technicians here will help you get that 'youthful' LA look.

Le Spa at the Sofitel Hotel, 8555 Beverly Blvd (La Cienega), West Hollywood

Tel: 310 228 6777   www.sofitel.com

Complimentary foot soaks before spa treatments and individual tea service make add a level of decadence to this already luxurious spa.

Los Angeles Massage Therapy Center, 2130 Sawtelle Blvd (Olympic), West Los Angeles

Tel: 310 444 8989   www.massagenow.com

This is massage therapy, not psychotherapy. Here, an hour means an hour – not 50 minutes. And each esthetician and massage therapist gets a 15-minute break between appointments. They're relaxed, so you're bound to be.

SPORTS CENTERS

Angel Stadium of Anaheim, 2000 Gene Autry Way (Orange Fwy), Anaheim

Tel: 714 940 2000   www.angels.mlb.com

This well-appointed stadium is home to the Los Angeles Angels of Anaheim. Fans of this minor league team tend to be more die-hard – and, frankly, interested in the game – than their counterparts just 25 miles to the north.

Dodger Stadium, 1000 Elysian Park Ave (Stadium Way) Elysian Park

Tel: 323 225 1690   www.dodgers.mlb.com

The most important rule to know in baseball? The stadium's bar limits alcohol purchases to two drinks per person at any given time. So if you're buying a round for your whole row, get a few friends to come with you.

Honda Center (formerly Arrowhead Pond of Anaheim), 2695 East Katella Ave (Orange Fwy), Anaheim
Tel: 714 704 2500 www.hondacenter.com

Just down the road from Disneyland, the Anaheim Ducks hockey team duke it out on the ice.

Staples Center, 111 S Figueroa Blvd (W 1st St), Downtown
Tel: 213 742 7100 www.staplescenter.com

Home to five professional sports franchises – the Lakers and Clippers basketball teams, ice hockey team the Kings, the arena football team the Avengers, and the Sparks women's basketball team – the Staples Center is also known for its rock concerts. (This is where U2 and Madonna play when they play LA.) And with five restaurants and a bevy of concession options, you're guaranteed to find more than typical fan fare. After all, nothing goes with hockey quite like sushi, right?

SURFING

Learn to Surf LA, various locations
Tel: 310 663 2479 www.learntosurfla.com

A favorite surf school in the Santa Monica, Manhattan, Malibu, and Zuma areas, this year-round surf school provides all the equipment and promises to get you catching waves in one lesson. A single class costs about $120 for one surfer and $200 for two.

Santa Monica Surf School, 2634 6th St (Ocean Park), Santa Monica
Tel: 310 526 3346 www.santammonicasurfschool.com

Specializing in private surf lessons, this school offers a 'starter package' for people who 'want a jumpstart on the basics of the sport.' The $305 package includes three two-hour lessons and equipment.

Surf Academy, various locations
Tel: 310 372 2790 www.surfacademy.org

Offering private lessons, group classes, and even 'Silver Surfer' instructions for surf virgins over 50, Surf Academy holds two-hour classes all along the coastline to teach you how to stand up on your board – and what to do when you wipe out. Prices vary, but run to about $50 for a single class.

Trapeze School New York, 370 Santa Monica Pier (Ocean), Santa Monica
Tel: 310 394 5800 losangeles.trapezeschool.com

Sunbathing too boring for you? Surfing too mundane? Then try flying through the ocean air with nothing but a net (several feet) beneath your feet. Single trapeze lessons are available at this outdoor 'school' on the Santa Monica Pier year-round. Prices $45–65 depending on the time and day of the week you choose to make your death-defying leap.

Los Angeles Zoo, 5333 Zoo Drive (Golden State Fwy), Griffith Park
Tel: 323 644 4200 www.lazoo.org
Open: daily, 10am–5pm

This small-ish zoo is easy to navigate and has a wonderful collection of animals, particularly primates. Time your trip carefully: mid-day visits can get hot in the summer, and zoo workers start putting animals away for the night at 4pm.

San Diego Wild Animal Park, 2920 Zoo Drive (Park), San Diego
Tel: 760 747 8702 www.sandiegozoo.org
Open: daily, 9am–4pm (8pm July/August)

San Diego has two, separate renowned zoos: the San Diego Zoo and the San Diego Wild Animal Park. Both are dizzyingly large and showcase animals in a fantastic, 'natural' way. For a completely unique experience, though, you're better off at the Wild Animal Park. From one of their Photo Caravan Safaris, you can feed giraffes and see eye to eye with rhinos. The park's special overnight tours even allow you to camp near lion country. Visiting the Wild Animal Park will feel like being on safari. But with a concession stand.

info...

DRESSING

We always hear about the famous balmy, sun-drenched days of Los Angeles. What many have come to discover upon arrival, however, is that it gets darn chilly at night, especially by the water (Venice, Santa Monica) and in the Hills. Come prepared with some light layers – a medium wait blazer or coat, a hooded zip-front sweatshirt, and perhaps a cotton crewneck sweater that can make you look respectable at the drop of a hat. Good jeans are a must, so leave your high-waisters at home and invest in some denim from Diesel, Joe's Jeans, or 7 For All Mankind. Now, the general population shies away from fancy or fussy dressing. Rather, it's about cool, casual comfort and subtle application of trends. A frequent faux pas made here is for folks to dress (how do we say this delicately?) age-inappropriately. Knowing this, feel empowered to show some skin. But don't forget who you are or where you come from… Stay classy, people.

DRIVING

People live in their cars here. Their automobiles are status symbols, extensions of their personalities, sanctuaries, escape hatches… The car culture, therefore, is pretty major. If you hail from a place where jaywalking is the norm, be warned… Doing so could result in a fine, and worse, the LA drivers aren't so used to it and they might take you out. As Woody Allen famously mentioned in *Annie Hall*, you can indeed turn right on a red light. Do watch for left hand turn regulations during rush hour (4pm and 7 p.m.).

MONEY

ATM machines aren't as ever-present as they are in other cities, though they certainly can be found. Check your bank's website if you can, or ask your host or concierge. Most establishments take credit and debit cards. Keep quarters handy in your car for metered parking, and have plenty of small change to tip your valets.

NAVIGATION

A good, clear map will really help you get around. Your car rental company will have decent maps to provide, though you may want to invest in one from

Streetwise, streetwisemaps.com. Or maybe pay the extra bucks for a GPS system. They're neat. Lay of the land, in short: Santa Monica, Venice, Brentwood, Westwood, and the Pacific Palisades are way west. Heading east: Bel Air and Beverly Hills, Century City and Culver City, West Hollywood, Mid Wilshire, and Midtown. Eastward still: Hollywood, Echo Park, Los Feliz, Silver Lake, and Glendale. Of course, if you head up the Pacific Cast highway a bit, you'll get to Malibu, ritzy, beachy, glitzy home to the stars.

PUBLIC HOLIDAYS

You haven't experienced Halloween until you've done so in West Hollywood. This town full of hams pulls out all the stops and takes to the streets in full regalia. Beyond that, here are the North American public holidays, according to the US bank holiday calendar: New Year's Day (January 1), Martin Luther King, Jr. Day (third Monday of January), President's Day (third Monday of February), Good Friday (Friday before Easter), Memorial Day (last Monday of May), Independence Day (July 4), Labor Day (first Monday in September), Columbus Day (October 12), Veteran's Day (November 11), Thanksgiving Day (fourth Thursday of November), Christmas Day (December 25).

PUBLIC TRANSPORTATION

There is a clean subway system that runs on the east side, though it's not going to help you if you plan on crisscrossing town. There is a great bus system that connects the city, though… Visit Metro.net to get a map. Expect the city to develop its public transportation system in the coming years.

SMOKING

While smoking looks mysterious and sexy in movies, it's not welcome inside bars, restaurants, and other public establishments, so you'll have to take your Kools, Gauloises, and Marlboros to the sidewalk. Many spots have courtyards and patios that are quite lovely, so you should be able to light up there. One thing… If you're sitting al fresco, be considerate of your neighbors… No one likes a mouthful of smoke while digging into a chopped salad.

info...

SOBRIETY RESOURCES

This is the Hedonist's Guide, but should you be in the market for a 12-Step meeting, visit lacoaa.org.

TAXIS/CAR SERVICES

It's not much of a walking city, so don't expect to hail a cab when you are in need. If you're out carousing and imbibing and can't responsibly drive yourself back to home base, don't! You don't want to get pulled over by the charming LAPD (like any number of young Hollywood stars) or, oh yeah, crash. Instead, keep a car service number handy. Ask your concierge or host, or use one of these: Bell Cab Hollywood (213 221 3800), Metro Cab (310 260 2747), and Lotus Taxi (310 393 5599).

TELEPHONES

To dial to Los Angeles from out of the country, dial 00 + 1 + 310 (or 323 or 213) before your number. If dialing from within the United States or Canada, simply dial 1 + 310 (or 323 or 213) and then your number.

TIPPING

Remember this when considering gratuities… Your servers are usually struggling, big-dreaming artists trying to catch a break. So generous tips are a great way to support the arts. .) For excellent service in a restaurant or bar, give 20 percent. For so-so service, the customary tip is 15 percent. For maid service, leave $3 for every time they clean the room. For hairdressers or massage therapists, give between 15 and 20 percent. For doormen, give a dollar. For valet, tip between $1 and $5.

Notes & Updates

Hg2 Los Angeles

index